The Stupidest Things Ever Said

BOOK OF
ALL-TIME STUPIDEST
TOP 10 LISTS

The Stupidest Things Ever Said

BOOK OF ALL-TIME STUPIDEST TOP 10 LISTS

KATHRYN AND ROSS PETRAS

Workman Publishing • New York

Library of Congress Cataloging-in-Publication Data
Petras, Kathryn.
 The stupidest things ever said : book of all-time stupidest top 10 lists /
 Kathryn & Ross Petras.
     p. cm.
 ISBN 978-0-7611-6591-0 (alk. paper)
 1. Stupidity—Humor. 2. American wit and humor.
 3. Wit and humor. I. Petras, Ross. II. Title.
PN6231.S77P47 2011
818'.5402—dc23   2011031528

Cover art by Robert Risko
Photo credits for interior art appear on page 232

Workman books are available at special discounts when purchased in
bulk for premiums and sales promotions as well as for fund-raising or
educational use. Special editions or book excerpts also can be created
to specification. For details, contact the Special Sales Director at the
address below, or send an e-mail to specialmarkets@workman.com.

WORKMAN PUBLISHING COMPANY, INC.
225 Varick Street
New York, NY 10014-4381
www.workman.com

Printed in the United States of America
First printing September 2011
10 9 8 7 6 5 4 3 2 1

CONTACT US

Heard a stupid thing?

Read a stupid thing?

Seen a stupid thing?

Know a stupid thing?

Send it to us!

We're always on the lookout for more stupidity for our books, calendar, and blog—so if you've got something to share, you can e-mail us:

teamstupidest@stupidest.com
stupidestcalendar@yahoo.com

or write us:

Ross & Kathryn Petras
STUPIDEST THINGS EVER SAID
Workman Publishing
225 Varick Street
New York, NY 10014

Or post it on our blog:

www.stupidest.com

And let us know if you want credit for your find.

ACKNOWLEDGMENTS

This collection of stupidity wouldn't have been possible without the help of our readers who've sent in so many truly stupid and wonderfully idiotic items over the years. Thanks to you all! We've tried to include the names of everyone who wanted to be credited (although we may have missed a few . . . the problem with collecting stupidity is that is seems to rub off a bit!). That said, special thanks to:

Blake Barrick, Rhea Baugher, Tom Berg, Ken Borland, Dave Boudreaux, Elaine Brown, Jason Cerar, Chris from Long Island, John Christian, Silvia Antonina Ciaccio, Miss L. Clayton, Dan Cousineau, Richard Dembrowski, Vicki Denny, Erica Derout, Craig Downey, Barrie Drain, Daniel Durchslag, Scott Eadie, Sarah Elan, Philo C. Farson, Glen Felson, Mike Fleice, Bob Given, Colin Griggs, Andrea Grody, V. Hazen, Bryson David Hoff, Judi Ieronimo, Matt Jenner, Jon Kolenchak, Emily Lauderdale, Crystal Lemcke, Larry Lesser, Bill Letson, Tanya Maes, Lin Malki, Scotland Miles, D.J. Mitchell, Todd Morgan, Richard Oberholzer, Paul and Leslie Patterson, Rev. David Peterson, Christa Poirier, Lawrence Ridley, Stu Roach, Larry Rogak, Steve Salinas, David Reed Staller, Tony and Jean Taffs, Dave Thayer, Buddy Truitt, Nathan White, Mrs. B. Williams, Betsy Wurm, Mike Yohe, Peter Zilliox, and the hundreds of other stupidity experts who prefer to remain nameless.

INTRODUCTION

On an April Sunday in 1993, at the close of his weekly television show, the famous, respected, serious, and poker-faced newsman David Brinkley read a few stupid quotes from our recently published book—*The 776 Stupidest Things Ever Said*—and actually laughed. For us, the rest was history.

The book took off and so began our career as professional stupidity collectors, writers, and compilers. It's been a lot of fun. Over the years we have read, listened to, and heard literally thousands of stupidities. Thousands of our readers have sent us their favorites as well. This book is the result, the crème de la crème of stupidity.

But what makes something one of the stupidest things ever said (or written, broadcast, produced, or otherwise disseminated—since early on we realized that to limit ourselves merely to things said would omit some true gems)? Well, sometimes it's unintended irony. Or a horribly inappropriate choice of words. Sometimes it's a mangled cliché, a bizarre analogy, a completely off-the-mark translation, a ridiculous misstatement, or an example of convoluted logic. You'll see all of this—and more—here.

We've arranged this collection of the stupidest of the stupidest into top 10 lists (as you may have guessed from the title . . .). And just as stupidity is boundless, so is the scope of the lists here. They're a wide-ranging, rather haphazard, but very intriguing collection (if we say so ourselves)—everything from "The Top 10 Stupidest Bee Comments" to "The Top 10 Stupidest Bureaucratic Blatherings."

So there you have it: a collection of the stupidest things ever said and more. A collection of the stupidities that made us laugh the most.

We loved putting this book together. We hope you laugh as much as we did.

Examples of Celebrities Sharing Their Vast Knowledge

1. Pericles? Is he the guy that did the thing with the potatoes?
>*actress Tara Reid*

2. **Radio host Howard Stern:** What is the capital of New York?
Actress Tori Spelling: New Jersey?

3. Who is Yom Kippur? Is that the name of the new Japanese designer?
>*model-turned-businesswoman Kathy Ireland*

4. I feel like a pilgrim from the f∗∗∗ing '20s washing this shit in the sink.
>Jersey Shore *reality star Snooki*

5. **Q:** Did you visit the Parthenon when you were in Greece?

Basketball star Shaquille O'Neil: I can't really remember the names of the clubs that we went to.

6. This [the threads in a $20 bill] is so the United States government can scan you. They can tell if you're carrying too much currency. When I showed this to my husband, it really wowed him. When I pulled out this little spy trick, he knew how well he'd done with me.

> *actress Patricia Arquette, during an* Us *magazine interview, in which she pulled out a $20 bill, ripped off a corner, and pointed out the threads in the bill to the reporter*

7. **Lawyer:** What was your companion's last name?
Socialite Paris Hilton: It is like a weird Greek name. Like Douglas.

8. **TV host Jon Stewart:** What is the capital of Uruguay?
Actor Lorenzo Lamas: There is no capital of Uruguay, you dummy—it's a country!

9. How can you get a volcano in Iceland? When you think of volcanos you think of Hawaii, or long words like that. You don't think of Iceland. It's too cold to have a volcano there.
> *CNN anchor Rick Sanchez*

10. **Q:** Who was the president during the Civil War?
Rocker Tommy Lee: Ummm . . . Winston Churchill? I wasn't around then, so who cares?
Q: What is an isosceles triangle?
Lee: Somewhere in Bermuda?
Q: What is pi?
Lee: Is that the 2 = MC squared thing?

Personal Introductions

1. A man I'm proud to call my friend. A man who will be the next president of the United States—Barack America!

> *Sen. Joe Biden, at his first campaign rally with Sen. Barack Obama*

2. Speaking of animals, he married his wife, Suzanne, when he was in college.

> *Utah governor Mike Leavitt,*
> *introducing Sen. Larry Craig*

3. My friends, it's with a great deal of pride that I present to you a president who wants to cut jobs—who wants to cut taxes to cut jobs—who wants to stop the regulations to cut the jobs . . . .

> *politician introducing President*
> *George Bush to an audience*

4. Hi, I'm Dean White, Dick of the college.

> *Duke University academic dean Richard (Dick) White,*
> *introducing himself at a faculty dinner*

5. *New York hostess introducing Russian Prince Yussupov, who participated in the killing of the "mad monk" Rasputin:*

This is Prince Yussupov, who murdered—just who was it you *did* murder, Prince Yussupov?

6. Here now is the Reverend Father McFadden—known all over the city, all over the country, all over the world and all over the . . . , all over the . . . , er, and other places besides.

> *British member of Parliament, introducing a special guest*

7. We're very proud to have Sugar Ray and Mrs. Ray here.

> *President Ronald Reagan, hosting Sugar Ray Robinson and wife*

8. This country needs a spearchucker, and I think we've got him up on this podium.

> *Kenosha, Wisconsin, mayor Eugene Dorff, introducing presidential candidate Jesse Jackson. (He said later he had intended to say "straight shooter," but slipped.)*

9. Stand up, Chuck, let 'em see ya!

> *Vice President Joe Biden to wheelchair-bound Missouri state senator Chuck Graham*

10. Here is Miss Monica Dickson to give you another talk on Cocking and Snooping—I beg your pardon—on Shocking and Cooping—er—I'm so sorry—Miss Monica Dickson . . .

> *television reporter Leslie Mitchell, attempting to introduce a guest who was going to talk about cooking and shopping*

Newspaper Corrections

1. Correction: Last week's column mistakenly misidentified a source. The European Commission president is Romano Prodi, not Buffy the Vampire Slayer.

> The Prague Post

2. A Nov. 9 Southan News story about Nova Scotia's black minority was accompanied by an inaccurate photograph caption. The photo, said to depict rundown homes outside Dartmouth, was actually of a pig farm. The *Citizen* apologises for the error.

> The Citizen *(Amherst, Canada)*

3. There was a typo in lawyer Ed Morrison's ad. His logo is: "Your case is no stronger than your attorney," not "stranger."

> Tulsa (Oklahoma) Gusher

4. Clarification: The phrase "Dummy Head," which was accidentally printed beneath a photograph in Thursday's *Clarion-Dispatch*, was intended as a typographical notation for use in the production process. It was not intended to describe in any way the subject of the photograph.

> Clarion-Dispatch *(Alaska)*

5. Norma Adams-Wade's June 15 column incorrectly called Mary Ann Thompson-Frenk a socialist. She is a socialite.

> The Dallas Morning News

6. The Denver Daily News would like to offer a sincere apology for a typo in Wednesday's Town Talk. . . . It was not the author's intention to call New Jersey "Jew Jersey."

> Denver Daily News

7. *The Daily Evergreen* would like to sincerely apologize for an injustice served to the Filipino-American, Spanish-speaking and Catholic communities on the front page of Thursday's Evergreen. The story "Filipino-American history recognized" stated that the "Nuestra Senora de Buena Esperanza," the galleon on which the first Filipinos landed at Morro Bay, Calif., loosely translates to "The Big Ass Spanish Boat." It actually translates to "Our Lady of Good Hope."

Washington State University's The Daily Evergreen

8. Current regrets describing the offices of NPR Ventures as "plush" in the March 25 issue. Although there is a couch in the reception area that could be described as plush, on closer inspection the offices proved to be just ordinary.

telecommunications magazine Current

9. Because of a reporting error, Dr. Arleigh Dygert Richardson III, former teacher at Lawrence Academy in Groton, was described in his obituary yesterday as favoring tacky pants with tweed jackets and Oxford shirts. Dr. Richardson favored khaki pants.

The Boston Globe

10. The following corrects errors in the July 17 geographical agent and broker listing: International: Aberdeen is in Scotland, not Saudi Arabia; Antwerp is in Belgium, not Barbados; Belfast is in Northern Ireland, not Nigeria; Cardiff is in Wales, not Vietnam; Helsinki is in Finland, not Fiji; Moscow is in Russia, not Qatar.

Business Insurance *magazine*

And Least Inspirational
Coaches and Managers

1. Just remember the words of Patrick Henry: "Kill me or let me live!"
   college football coach Bill Peterson

2. We might not be big enough, but it's the size of the dog in the fight
   or the fight of the size in the fog. . . . Whatever it is, we don't got it.
   *basketball coach Mike D'Antoni, commenting on his team's terrible
   starting record*

3. We've got a good squad and we're
   going to cut our cloth accordingly.
   But I think the cloth we've got
   could make some good soup, if
   that makes any sense.
   soccer coach Ian Holloway

4. Basketball develops
   individuality, initiative and
   leadership. Now get out there
   and do exactly what I tell
   you to.
   *college basketball coach
   Dick Vitale*

5. We're not as good as we think we are.
   We need to go out there and prove that!
   soccer manager Steve McClaren

6. **Reporter:** Is there anything this team does well?
Basketball coach: Not really.
Reporter: Are you making any progress?
Coach: I couldn't truthfully say that we are.
Reporter: Do you like coaching the team?
Coach: I don't care that much for basketball.

*interview with the coach of the Friendsville
Academy Foxes basketball team, which had chalked up
128 consecutive losses*

7. I do not believe that at this moment in time, if that changes in years to come I don't know, but what happens here today and changes as we go along that is part of life's learning and part of your inner beliefs.

soccer manager Glenn Hoddle

8. I want 100 minutes of 60 percent football.

college coach John Potsklan

9. You guys start doing your warm-ups, and when I'm ready for you [holding up whistle] I'll blow you.

college football coach John Potsklan

10. And I honestly believe we can go all the way to Wembley . . . unless somebody knocks us out.

soccer coach Dave Bassett

Least Comprehensible Advertising Slogans Ever Written

1. Be half as fresh as the day is long

    on tampon package, Japan

2. Ghana, is, as you perhaps in Korea, and is regarded as the high-qualified Ghana our marvelous, smooth and mild whole already know, enjoying high reputation selling chocolates masterpieces of all milk chocolate.

    on wrapper of Ghana brand chocolate bar, Korea

3. Men's Under Wear:

We'll advise you about your "stickiness" about your daily life.

    on men's underwear tag, Japan

4. Nobody can come to the Medusa Business Club.

    in ad for the oddly named club, Ho Chi Minh City (Saigon), Vietnam

5. Everyone has different personality and taste. If they get together, it makes a family. "Every" is always staying near our life.

    on Mitsubishi microvan "Every Joy Pop Turbo" models, Japan

6. We Try Our Best to Decrease Your Life
in shop window, China

7. Train

<u>+ Ing</u>

Traing
on posters for East Japan Railway Company, posted throughout stations and famous among English-speaking visitors, who can't figure out what it's supposed to mean

8. Shangri-la is in your mind but your buffalo is not.
on billboard, China

9. Smart noshery makes you slobber
on restaurant sign, Shanghai, China

10. Too fast to live, too young to happy
on cream soda bottle, Japan

Religiously Ridiculous Remarks

1. Sunday's Lifestyle story about Buddhism should have stated that Siddhartha Gautama grew up in Northern India, not Indiana.

> Bloomington (Indiana) Herald-Times

2. **Realmente Bella Señorita Panamá beauty pageant judge:** Explain the Confucius quote "Learning without thought is labor lost."

Contestant Giosué Enith Cozzarelli Sanmartín: Good evening, Panama. Confucius was one of whom invented confusion and that's why, uhh . . . One of the most ancient, he was one of the Chinese . . . Japanese who were one of the most ancient. Thank you.

3. **Woman in grocery store:** Is this matzoh kosher for passover?
Salesperson: Oh, don't worry about it. You can just take it to your priest and he'll bless it for you.

4. Presbyterian Church Easter Sunday Denver Colorado
Call to Worship
Pastor: Christ has risen!
People: Christ has risen indeed.
Pastor: Joe is alive!
People: Redemption is here.

> *in a church bulletin*

5. If the Apostle Paul had been here Saturday . . . he would have enjoyed seeing the Wisconsin-Iowa football game.

> *Rev. A. J. Soldan, pastor of the Luther Memorial Church in Madison, Wisconsin, 1926*

6. *Are You Smarter Than a 10 Year Old?* **host:** According to the Old Testament, on which mountain did Moses receive the Ten Commandments?

Contestant: Ah, I think I know this one. Something tells me it's Mount Rushmore.

7. **Documentary maker Alexandra Pelosi:** What sort of car would Jesus have driven?

Driving club member, Cruisers for Christ: He might have driven a Chrysler.

8. Here is an evening prayer for the little ones, and to me it is very sweet and solemn:

Savior, tender Shepherd, hear me,
Bless thy little lamb tonight,
In the darkness be Thou near me,
Keep me safe till morning light.
To remove rust from window glass, dip
cloth in coal oil and rub hard.

The Kansas City (Missouri) Star

9. If Christ were a ballplayer, he'd be the best there was. He'd take out the guy at second base, then he'd say, "I love you," pick him up, slap him on the butt and come back to the dugout.

baseball player Brett Butler

10. We'd like to have Baptist ministers and Catholic priests buying and selling drugs, but the real world doesn't operate that way.

John Paschall, the Robertson County (Texas) district attorney, commenting on drug arrests and defending the credibility of informer Derrick Megress

Lamest Excuses and Explanations That Don't Quite Cut It

1. *Appearing in court on a charge of soliciting prostitutes:*
When I said I wanted head, I meant I wanted to get inside the head of the prostitute to do a news story.

newscaster Harry Trout of Baltimore (he was acquitted)

2. *After being charged with indecent exposure after he was caught walking down the street naked at 4:30 A.M. and telling police he had been jogging at the Frederick, Colorado, high school track:*

I'm a heavy man, and wearing clothing while running makes me sweat profusely.

Rev. Robert Whipkey, Colorado

3. *When several photos of him wearing a Nazi Waffen SS uniform surfaced:*

I've always been fascinated by the fact that here was a relatively small country that from a strictly military point of view accomplished incredible things.

Republican nominee for Congress from Ohio's 9th District Rich Iott

4. *When asked if she was asleep during a speech by Al Gore:*

No. I'm going through eye exercise therapy, strengthening my eyes. I'm supposed to . . . like, rest them.

> *lifestyle expert Martha Stewart*

5. *Responding to a charge by a Nuclear Regulatory Commission inspector that two Dresden nuclear plant operators were sleeping on the job:*

It depends on your definition of asleep. They weren't stretched out. They had their eyes closed. They were seated at their desks with their heads in a nodding position.

> *Commonwealth Edison, Illinois, supervisor of news information John Hogan*

6. *Referring to rumors that a woman had been attacked by a shark while swimming at the beach:*

It wasn't a shark attack, but a shark *accident*. More than likely he ran into [the swimmer's] leg and got it caught in his mouth.

> *South Padre Island, Texas, town spokesman Joe Rubio*

7. **Brazilian representative, in charge of an investigation alleging abuses concerning the national budget:** Mr. Alves, how do you explain the money found in your bank account?

Rep. Joao Alves, accused of heading up the budget misuse: It's my money.

Investigator: But can you please explain to us how you made this kind of money?

Aves: Easy. I won it all in lottery tickets. I won 125 times in the last two years.

8. *After being caught in the Miami airport returning from a ten-day trip to Europe with a hired male prostitute:*

I had surgery and I can't lift luggage. That's why I hired him.

> *antigay crusader and cofounder of the Family Research Council Rev. George Rekers*

9. *After a woman found a mouse's foot in a jar of Slovenian pickles:*

It is completely normal in big factories to have mice wandering around, and yes, every now and then they get caught amongst the machines and do get bottled, seasoned, preserved and even make it in one piece to consumers. Although not very pleasant to see, however, they pose no health threat at all. During the preservation process even traces of any salmonella bacteria are eliminated in food. A mice-foot therefore could be classified as a special additive to the pickles.

> *Slovenian Health Ministry spokeswoman Vivijan Potocnik*

10. *When accused of inappropriate behavior at a strip club:*

First, it was not a strip bar, it was an erotic club. And, second, what can I say? I'm a night owl.

> *Washington, D.C., mayor Marion Barry*

Existentially Peculiar Road Signs

1. The Slippery Are Very Crafty

> *Chinese road sign literally translated into English—it's supposed to mean "Caution: Wet Roads"*

2. Entering Dieback Uninterpretable

> *road sign in Perth, Australia, regarding dieback, a tree disease*

3. Be Aware of Invisibility

> *sign on road to Ngorongoro Crater, Tanzania*

4. No more. Please pack up now.

> *road sign by dead-end in Istanbul, Turkey*

5. Permitted vehicles not allowed

> *orange temporary road sign on side of US 27, Florida Entrance Lane*

6. Danger: High Voltage for Your Safety

> *sign on London street*

7. When this sign is under water, this road is impassable.

> *sign on Tennessee highway*

8. Danger Ahead

Fasten Safety Belts

And Remove Dentures

> *road sign in Namibia*

9. Stop: Drive Sideways

> *detour sign in Kyushi, Japan*

10. Changed Priorities Ahead

> *road sign in England*

Double Entendres

1. Student Excited Dad Got Head Job

headline, The University Daily Kansan

2. At night the flavour changes as Turkish women don't tend to come out at night. Their absence has probably got something to do with the awful organ music that seems so popular here. It takes little persuasion for another tone deaf Turk to leap up in a lokanta and wildly pump his organ, singing incomprehensible words in between gasps for air.

from a travel article on Turkey, Lancaster Travel

3. Tiger Woods Plays With Own Balls, Nike Says

headline, Associated Press

4. The wedding was consummated in the garden of the American Consul's home in the presence of more than a hundred distinguished guests.

The Japan Times

5. You must have had some famous players come through your hands over the years. [pause] I think I'll rephrase that.

TV sportscaster in an on-air interview

6. Gators to Face Seminoles with Peters Out

headline, Tallahassee (Florida) Bugle

7. The rather beautiful-looking mulberry bush behind me is approximately 400 years old and it's said that it's one of the finest examples around. One other that you can see, if you're lucky enough, is in the grounds of Buckingham Palace. But apparently, this is much bigger, much grander, than the Queen's bush.

British television feature reporter

8. Tony has a quick look between his legs and likes what he sees.

horse-racing announcer Stewart Machin, about jockey Tony McCoy

9. From his emergency flood headquarters at City Hall, Mayor Friedman has just ordered all families living near or adjacent to the Mill River to ejaculate immediately.

WLKW-TV (Rhode Island) news director, delivering an emergency news bulletin on-air

10. Local man's sauce puts some "spunk" into food

headline, South Bend (Indiana) Tribune

Impossible-to-Follow Instructions

1. If you cannot read these directions and warnings, do not use this product.

label on a bottle of drain cleaner

2. Final grid entries corresponding to the asterisked clues can be paired to form anagrams of a sequence of names, with one missing. To achieve this solvers must change one unchecked letter in each pair of the corresponding answers, forming new words. Corrected single letter misprints in the definitions of 15 clues in order, followed by the unjumbled 3 down, spell out the thematic position.

Half of the clued answers are to be entered in reverse and all thematic names consist of two words (one hyphenated). The missing names can be formed from the final letters in the shaded squares and this must be written below the grid. Chambers (2008) is recommended, but only gives 10 down in conjunction with its direction.

instructions for a crossword puzzle in Cambridge University's alumni magazine Cam

3. Emergency Instructions: Helpsavering apparata in emergings behold many whistles! Associate the stringing apparata about the bosoms and meet behind. Flee then to the indifferent lifesaving shippen obediencing the instructs of the vessel chef.

> *sign posted on a Russian ship in the Black Sea*

4. Can you hear me? Squeeze once for yes and twice for no.

> *police detective, questioning a wounded officer*

5. Temporarily each of you, four players, represent a side and the very same man picks up the dice and throws once so as to see who is going to represent the temporary east and so on. If the number of points are 3,7,11 the man opposite the East, the West, if 2,6,10 the man on the right or the South, if 4,8, 12, the man on the left, the North, and if 5, or 9 the East himself starts drawing the topmost Position Indicator, the second, third and fourth by the south, west and north in their respective order and turn (counter clockwise). In turning over the Indicator each one of you will find where you are to be seated. By this simple process, the allotment of seats is determined.

> *instructions on seating players, included in a Mah-jongg game from China*

6. All ice cubes will be boiled before using.

> *U.S. army official, ordering preventative measures during an overseas typhoid epidemic*

7. This is a test of the email system at OPPD. If you get this message, call me at ext. 3848. If you don't get this message, then call me at ext. 3886.

> *sent by the help desk to workers at the Omaha Public Power District after workers had reported problems with the e-mail system*

8. Hold B about 3 seconds then push B once or push B once by once

(Day of week flag above Tuesday flashing)

Select flashing digit(s) to be set by push C or A

Advance figure by pushing A or C

Select 12/24 hour cycle option in normal time

Hold A then push B or when time (hour) setting. 12/24

hour cycle option will appear alternately on every 24

hour cycle during hour advance Month and date

interchange by holding C then push A or cannot be changed.

> *from the instruction manual for a stopwatch made in China*

9. No trespassing without permission.

> *sign on the grounds of a public school*

10. Please burn before reading.

> *1972 Nixon White House memo on illegal campaign tactics being planned against Democratic candidate George McGovern*

Painfully Truthful Things Said by Politicians

1. You're so damned concerned with what the public thinks that it gets in the way of what's best for *us*!

> *Vista, California, city council member Jeanette Smith, responding to other council members who were against holding a dinner meeting that would be paid for by the public*

2. You had some good points. It was kind of long, so I forgot some of them.

> *Louisiana state senator Diana Bajoie (D-New Orleans), during a debate*

3. If this trend continues, no one could discriminate against anyone for any reason!

> *Republican delegate Kelli Sobonya (Cabell County, West Virginia), speaking against extending a human rights law to cover homosexuals and the disabled*

4. Q: What has been the most important legislation passed in this session?

Florida state senator Mallory Horne: Well, passed . . . uh, you'd have to . . . uh, really, say that most of it at this juncture is, uh, still in the wings. Um, we have, uh, hold that a minute, I can't think of a darn thing we've passed.

5. My problem was, I was too honest with you the first time.

> *Rep. Tillie Fowler (R-Florida) to her constituents, explaining why she had changed her mind about term limits*

6. I've had just about all of this good government stuff I can stand.

Louisiana state senator Charles Jones (D-Monroe), during a debate in the Louisiana State Legislature

7. My colleagues and I are upset by this blatant attempt to replace diversity with fairness.

Joseph Doria, Democratic leader in the New Jersey State Assembly, on a bill repealing racial and gender preferences, as quoted in the New Jersey Law Journal. *(Not surprisingly, he later denied saying this.)*

8. We have to raise the car-rental tax as high as we can possibly do it. . . . We have to look at opportunities like that just to screw them [visitors].

Salt Lake City mayoral candidate Jim Bradley, explaining his thoughts on how to welcome visitors to the 2002 Winter Olympics in Salt Lake City

9. We're not able to tax people as much as we would like to.

Macon (Georgia) mayor Jack Ellis, talking about how low-income housing projects depend on both public and private funding

10. Hattie, I'm horny.

Arizona governor Bruce Babbitt, to his wife during his Democratic presidential campaign (he didn't realize the microphone was on)

THE TOP 10 STUPIDEST

Sportscaster
On-Air Moments

1. Winfield goes back to the wall. He hits his head on the wall and it rolls off! It's rolling all the way back to second base! This is a terrible thing for the Padres!

> *sportscaster Jerry Coleman, attempting to tell radio listeners about a fly ball hit by a member of the opposing team*

2. Wow . . . if only a face could talk.

> *sportscaster John Madden, during Super Bowl XXXI*

3. Owen runs like rabbit chasing after—what do rabbits run after? They run after nothing! Well, running after other rabbits.

> *sportscaster Tom Tyrell*

4. That's a sharply hit single into the left field and Greg Luzinksi hurries over to stop it from going into the gap in left center. The runner is rounding third and they're waving him on to score! Boone, the Phillies catcher, braces himself for collision at the plate. It's gonna be close! Oh, no! Schmidt cut off Luzinski's balls . . . Ball!

> *WCAU-Philadelphia sportscaster, on-air during a Phillies game*

5. It's gold or nothing . . . and it's nothing! He comes away with a silver medal.

  sportscaster David Coleman

6. So that's 24 points for Schumacher and 23 points for Hill—so there's only one point between them if my mental arithmetic is correct.

  sportscaster Murray Walker

7. Sportscaster #1: Hurst has been playing with a bulging dick, disc in his neck.

  Sportscaster #2: You've got to come up with better shit than that.

  Sportscaster #1: Is this live?

8. I have a feeling that, if she had been playing against herself, she would have won that point.

  sportscaster Bob Hewitt, covering a tennis match

9. It's now 1–1, an exact reversal of the score on Saturday.

  radio sportscaster, during live coverage of a game

10. And the ball is out here. No, it's not. Yes, it is. No, it's not. What happened?

  sportscaster Phil Rizzuto

Not-So-Catchy Song Titles

1. "The Joy of Bumper Harvest Overflows Amidst the Song of Mechanisation"

> *song title, North Korea*

2. "Music to Light Your Pilot By"

> *special recording put together by Heil-Quaker Corporation, heater and air conditioner manufacturer*

3. "Eternal Engine of Linguistic Massacre"

> *song title from CD of the soundtrack of a Japanese game called Valkyrie Profile, Japan*

4. "What for Are We Living Until We Die? Only Mr. God Knows Why."

> *song title, Latvia*

5. "The Shoes My Brother Bought Fit Me Tight"

> *song title, North Korea*

6. "I'm Vasectomized"

> *song title, Thailand*

7. "Drop Kick Me Jesus Through the Goalposts of Life"

> *country song title*

8. "Mother, I want to Go to the Mountainside and Harden Myself with Physical Labor"

> *song title, China*

9. "A Big Rabbit of our Sub Branch"

> *song title, North Korea*

10. "When the Party Is Over, I Miss My Dear Porn Star"

> *song title, China*

Newspaper Typos Ever Printed

1. Dear Abby:

I have a friend who has been seeing a guy who's been married, divorced and has five kids. She's so wrapped up in him that sometimes she doesn't see her family for weeks. Recently she told me that she loves this guy, but she wants to Baste ham or poultry with leftover syrup from canned fruit.

from a "Dear Abby" column appearing in a Tuscaloosa, Alabama, newspaper

2. Asked his conception of the Navy's role in a future war, Morrison picked up his book. "As certain as night succeeds the day, without a decisive navoin oiniou oiuiouiouoo ing definitive," he read. "Know who wrote that?"

The Patriot Ledger *(Quincy, Massachusetts)*

3. "I's very happy," said Olga, a medical student, in perfect English.

The Lynchburg (Virginia) Daily Advance

4. His comments followed claims that the Prince has been secretly Mrs. Parker-Bowles for more than a decade, and as often as once a week.

The (London) Evening Gazette

5. He smiled and let his gaze fall to hers, so that her cheek began to glow. Ecstatically she waited until his mouth slowly neared her own. She knew only one thing: rdoeniadtrgoveniardgoverdgovnrdgog.

Badische Presse

6. Although Sassoon did not die until 1967, it is his war poems for which he is best remembered. In 1918 he produced "Counter Attack," a fierce attack on all concerned with the war, except for the fighting hen.

The Daily Telegraph *(UK)*

7. Eight candidates, including all four incompetents, are seeking the four City Council positions.

The Cheney (Washington) Free Press

8. After his speech, the governor, accompanied by six children, his entourage and dozens of reporters, climbed out of his pool to pace along his chain-link fence, occasionally standing on his hind legs and tilting his head back.

Los Angeles Times

9. Several of the Rev. Dr. Mudge's friends called upon him yesterday, and after a conversation the unsuspecting pig was seized by the hind leg, and slid along a beam until he reached the hot-water tank. . . . Thereupon he came forward and said that there were times when the feelings overpowered one, and for that reason he would not attempt to do more than thank those around him for the manner in which such a huge animal was cut into fragments was simply astonishing.

The doctor concluded his remarks, when the machine seized him and in less time than it takes to write it the pig was cut into fragments and worked up into delicious sausage. The occasion will be long remembered by the doctor's friends as one of the most delightful of their lives. The best pieces can be procured for tenpence a pound, and we are sure that those who have sat so long under his ministry will rejoice that he has been treated so handsomely.

from an English newspaper in the late 1800s, when two stories—one on a patent pig-killing and sausage-making machine and the other on the Rev. Dr. Mudge being presented with a gold-headed cane—were mistakenly pieced together by typographers

10. The court said the operation of [the massage parlors] has been declared to be a pubic nuisance.

Nashville (Tennessee) Banner

Possibly Logical but Rather Awkward New Word Creations

1. Okay, everyone, now inhale . . . and then dehale!

> *baseball player Maury Wills, leading his teammates through warm-up calisthenics*

2. Our phenoms aren't phenomenating.

> *baseball manager Lefty Phillips, explaining why his team was having a bad year*

3. They misunderestimated me.

> *President George W. Bush*

4. Kimi Raikkonen, if not disgruntled, is certainly looking less than gruntled.

> *auto-racing commentator James Allen*

5. Ground Zero Mosque supporters: doesn't it stab you in the heart, as it does ours throughout the heartland? Peaceful Muslims, pls refudiate.

> *politician Sarah Palin, in a Twitter about plans to build an Islamic community center near Ground Zero*

6. In other words, feediness is the shared information between toputness where toputness is at a time just prior to the inputness.

> *U.S. Office of Education official report*

7. This is unparalyzed in the state's history.

> *Texas Speaker of the House Gib Lewis*

8. The knee feels fine, I've been training confuciously.

> *boxer Mike Tyson, talking about his comeback*

9. We had four must-win games and we musted.

> *pitcher Curt Schilling*

10. No, you're not going to see me stay put . . . I'm not going to forsake my responsibility. You may not see me put as much—I mean, un-put as much.

> *President George H. W. Bush, explaining his travel plans for the next year*

Bureaucratic Blatherings

1. This document did not concern you. Please erase your initials and initial your erasure.

U.S. Army personnel department, Fort Baker

2. Because of the Veterans Day holiday next Wednesday, this release will be published on Friday, November 13, instead of on Thursday, November 12. It will be issued on Thursday, November 19, its usual publication date, but will be delayed the following week until Friday, November 17, because of the Thanksgiving Day holiday on Thursday, November 26.

Federal Reserve memo

3. A Leap Year is determined if the 4-digit year can be divided by 4, Unless

The year can be divided by 100, then it is not a Leap Year, Unless

The year can be divided by 400, then it is a Leap Year, Unless

The year can be divided by 4000, then it is not a Leap Year, Unless

The year is 200 or 600 year after a year that is divisible by 900, then it is Leap Year.

memo put out by the Ohio Department of Administrative Services

4. Rat complaints have gone up, but we look at that as a *positive* thing, because more people know how to contact us now.

New York City complaints hotline bureaucrat

5. If the United States is attacked, file this page in book III of FPM Supplement 990-1, in front of part 771.

Effective upon an attack on the United States and until further notice: a. Part 771 is suspended.

from the "Federal Personnel Manual, Manual Supplement 990-3,
Civil Service Commission. Part M-771, Employee Grievances
and Appeals"

6. After a thorough investigation, we are able to determine that the late arrival of your mail was due to a delay in transit.

postal service reply to a complaint

7. *FUN FACTS FOR CHILDREN:*

DUF6 Cylinder Weight Comparisons A Ticonderoga-class cruiser is about equal in weight to 706 cylinders of depleted uranium hexafluoride (DUF6). It would take over 70 cruisers to weigh more than the Nation's inventory of DUF6! The Navy owns only 27 Ticonderoga-class cruisers. DUF6 Cylinder Weight Comparisons 7,142 cylinders of DUF6 weighs as much as a Nimitz-class aircraft carrier. The entire inventory of 57,634 cylinders weighs more than all eight of the Navy's Nimitz-class aircraft carriers combined!

from a U.S. Department of Energy website

8. Did you give consent for someone to steal or damage your property?

Yes ( ) No ( )

on a citizen self-reporting form from the Madison (Wisconsin)
Police Department

9. Due to an administrative error, the original of the attached letter was forwarded to you. A new original has been accomplished and forwarded to AAC/JA (Alaskan Air Command, Judge Advocate office). Please place this copy in your files and destroy the original.

memo from the Alaska Air Command

10. Associate Assistant Secretary

Assistant Assistant Secretary

Deputy Assistant Assistant Secretary

Associate Deputy Assistant Secretary

Chief of Staff to the Associate Assistant Secretary

Chief of Staff to the Assistant Assistant Secretary

Principal Deputy to the Deputy Assistant Secretary

Principal Assistant Deputy Undersecretary

Associate Principal Deputy Assistant Secretary

federal job titles, as quoted in The New York Times

Celebrity Literary Observations

1. *Rolling Stone* **interviewer:** What was the best thing you read all year?

Singer Justin Timberlake: You mean like a book?

2. I'm astounded by people who take 18 years to write something. That's how long it took that guy to write *Madame Bovary*, and was that ever on the best-seller list?

> *actor Sylvester Stallone*

3. When I was in prison I was wrapped up in all those deep books. That Tolstoy crap. People shouldn't read that stuff.

> *boxer Mike Tyson, on what he read before he decided he preferred comic books*

4. **Reporter:** Have you read the original Shakespearean version of the *Othello*?

Actor Lawrence Fishburne (who was acting in a modernized version of *Othello*): Why should I read all those words that I'm not going to get to say?

5. **Acting coach:** What about doing some Shakespeare?

Singer Britney Spears: I know who he is, know he's dead and I don't want any knights-in-armor stuff.

Acting coach [later]: Can you read from this Harold Pinter play?

Spears: No. Whoever Pinto is, or was.

6. I haven't read a book in my life. I haven't got enough time . . . I do love fashion magazines.

singer/model Victoria Beckham

7. I think that Shakespeare is a shit. Absolute shit! He may have been a genius for his time, but I just can't relate to that stuff. "Thee and thous"—the guy sounds like a faggot.

rocker Gene Simmons

8. I couldn't care less about all those fiction stories about what happened in the year 1500 or 1600. Half of them aren't even true.

golfer John Daly, explaining why he wasn't interested in literature as a college student

9. I'm a great fan of hers [writer Iris Murdoch's], but I haven't read any of her books.

actress Kate Winslet, who played young Iris Murdoch in the film Iris

10. I am not a fan of books. I would never want a book's autograph.

singer Kanye West

THE TOP 10 STUPIDEST
Restaurant Menu Items
for Carnivores

1. French fries—deep fried French people
menu item, Indonesia

2. Roasted Banker and Cream Sauce
menu item, Hiking Restaurant, Shanghai, China

3. Cowboy Leg
menu item, China

4. Lawyer Shrimps Salad
menu item, France

5. Nordic Salad: tomatoes, rice, salmon pish, grawn, superhuman
menu item, France

6. Genetal Tso's Chicken
menu item, New Jersey

7. Muscles of Marines
menu item, Egypt

8. Green people with beef fried rice
menu item, Hsin Chu, Taiwan

9. Tenderloin of Pork Merchant, Vegetables
menu item, Thai Airways

10. Cold shredded children and sea blubber in spicy sauce
menu item, Wan Chai, China

Statements That Will Make Men Uncomfortable

1. Allisonville Nursery
Where Home and Garden Meet
Fresh Cut Penis—$7.99

> *sign at an Indianapolis nursery (which was supposed to say "peonies" and was later corrected)*

2. Tomorrow on *Good Morning Virginia*, a Virginia classic from Bob Corey—fresh roasted penis!

> *newscaster Tab O'Neal, WSET-TV, Lynchburg, Virginia*

3. It's Summer Time! Bring your children to the Garma Specialty Clinic for Circumcision. (Children and Adult). Painless. Bloodless. German Cut.

> *newspaper ad, Manila, Philippines*

4. Ham on penis

> *menu item, Poland*

5. I was a victim of circumcision!

> *Pirates pitching coach Pete Vuckovich, after being ejected from a game*

6. Penis with chicken and curry

sign on a Mexico hotel buffet

7. Wimbledon hero Tim Henman has sold his balls, a snip at £25 a piece, to raise cash for the homeless.

South London Press

. . . And 3 That Will Make Women Wince

8. Beaver Condiments, $1.99—Horseradish, Cocktail Sauce, or Mustard

from a Lins Grocery (Western Family brand) flyer, Utah

9. Door Bell with Birth Sound

label on a bird-song doorbell chime, Japan

10. We Will Do Your Mom for Nothing

"Again & Again"

On Mother's Day

restaurant ad, Castine, Maine

Least Complimentary Compliments

1. She really has become a monster . . . I mean monster in the most positive way.

> *businessman Donald Trump, speaking about his then-pregnant wife, Melania*

2. Clinton's an unusually good liar. Unusually good. Do you realize that?

> *Sen. Bob Kerrey (D-Nebraska), in an* Esquire *interview*

It was an unfortunate remark that once it's in print it looks a lot worse than it actually is.

> *Sen. Bob Kerrey, commenting on his* Esquire *interview to AP*

It was not an angry comment. It was actually intended as an off-handed compliment.

> *Sen. Bob Kerrey, further explaining to UPI*

3. How complicated and mysterious he is. He's also a pseudo-intellectual, which is really interesting.

> *actress Melanie Griffith, talking about her husband, actor Antonio Banderas*

4. Alex Ferguson is the best manager I've ever had at this level. Well, he's the only manager I've actually had at this level.

> *soccer player David Beckham*

5. Ladies and gentlemen, it is my honor to introduce you to the governor of this great state, the Honorable John J. McKeithen and his lovely wife, Marjorie. Look how beautiful she is—every wrinkle in her face is glowing.

> *New Orleans mayor Vic Schiro, introducing the governor and his wife to the city council during a meeting*

6. They're the second best team in the world and there's no higher praise than that.

> *soccer manager Kevin Keegan*

7. This is a terrific script. It just needs a complete rewrite.

> *director Peter Bogdanovich to screenwriter Alvin Sargent, upon reading a draft of* Paper Moon

8. I mean, you got the first mainstream African-American who is articulate and bright and clean and a nice-looking guy. I mean, that's a storybook, man.

> *Sen. Joe Biden (D-Delaware), on fellow presidential candidate Sen. Barack Obama*

9. Dear Friends,

We are happy to be able to tell you, and we are sure that you will be proud to learn, that your son is now an Advanced Non-Swimmer.

> *letter from California camp authorities to parents*

10. There's no end to your limitations, Stephanie.

> *game show host Bob Eubanks to Stephanie Edwards during the 2006 Tournament of Roses telecast*

Cow-Related Commentary

1. Mad cow talks
   headline, Huddersfield Daily Examiner *(UK)*

2. Enraged Cow Injures Farmer with Axe
   headline, The Northern Echo *(UK)*

3. A cow may be drained dry; and if the Chancellors of the Exchequer persist in meeting every deficiency that occurs by taxing the brewing and distilling industries, they will inevitably kill the cow that lays the golden milk.
   British member of Parliament Frederick Milner

4. You don't look like my ex-wife at all. She was well-bred and rather frail, except for her famous mammalia. You look more like a cow than my late wife. Oh, no offense. I'm very fond of cows. Moooooo!
   Robert Mitchum to Liz Taylor, in Secret Ceremony *(1968)*

5. *Written on an insurance claim form by a claimant whose car hit a cow:*

   Q: What warning was given by you?

   A: Horn.

   Q: What warning was given by the other party?

   A: Moo.

6. His motion is slow only because he is of aslitudinous [*sic*] species. Also his other motion is much useful to trees, plants as well as making flat cakes in hand and drying in the sun. Cow is the only animal that extracates [*sic*] his feeding after eating. Then, afterward she chew with his teeth whom are situated in the inside of the mouth. He is incessantly in the meadows on the grass. He has got tail also, but not like similar animals. It has hairs on the other end of the other side.

This is the cow.

essay written by a candidate for the Indian Civil Service

7. Grain-consuming animal units—cows

U.S. Department of Agriculture definition

8. Stop, cow! Stop!

NYPD officers chasing a 100-pound calf that leaped from a slaughterhouse-bound truck and ran down the street. (The calf was later shipped to an upstate farm.)

9. Tonya Lynn Bruno and Mark Anthony Eagen will exchange wedding cows August 21 at St. Mary's Catholic Church

from an Idaho newspaper weddings announcement page

10. I was thrown from the car as it left the road. I was later found in a ditch by some stray cows.

courtroom testimony

THE TOP 10 STUPIDEST
(But Clearly Vital)
Police Blotter Reports

1. In Portola, a caller reported that while she was in the shower, someone snuck into her house and vomited on her stove. A deputy reported that it appeared to be cooking grease on the stove.

Portola (California) Reporter

2. Dog Attack—Lower Duck Pond, Lithia Park, Ashland. Police responded to a report of two dogs running loose and attacking ducks at about 11:20 A.M. Saturday.

The officer cited a resident for the loose dogs. The duck refused medical treatment and left the area, according to police reports.

Ashland (Oregon) Daily Tidings

3. Donuts were reported loitering in a field on Opening Hill Road.

police blotter item

4. Mountain View Friday Wal-Mart: Police receive a report of a newborn infant found in a trash can. Upon investigation, officers discover it was only a burrito.

California newspaper

5. Personnel at the Farmers First Bank on N. Cedar Street reported at 10:15 A.M. on May 13th the discovery of a mound of hair on May 10th.

> Lancaster (Pennsylvania) Intelligencer Journal

6. A police officer . . . found 17 clear plastic bags between two parked cars. Fourteen bags appeared to contain cocaine, and three appeared to contain marijuana, police reported. . . . If the drugs belong to you, call the detective bureau at 420-2106.

> Hoboken (New Jersey) Reporter

7. Saturday, Jan. 22: A staff member in Thackeray Hall reported to campus police that a male came into his office and began a conversation.

> *University of Pittsburgh newspaper*

8. Tree down, 5:45 P.M.: The sheriff's department reported a tree lying unconscious in the road on Carpenterville Road.

> *Oregon newspaper*

9. Deputies responded to reports of a gaggle of elk loitering in a public roadway creating a traffic hazard, near milepost 33, Highway 41, in Oldtown at 1:23 A.M. Deputies spoke with the elk and they agreed to leave the roadway and not return.

> *Idaho newspaper*

10. Belcoo police seized 20 cattle and 30 small pigs on suspicion of having been smuggled, assisted by Miss K. McDermott (violin) and Mrs. P. O'Rourke (percussion and effects).

> Fermanagh Herald *(Ireland)*

Similes, Muddled Metaphors, and Confused Clichés

1. He's not the sharpest sandwich in the picnic.
  sportscaster Tony Cascarino

2. You cannot change the stripes of a leopard.
  football player turned analyst Emmitt Smith

3. You can lead a dead horse to water, but you can't make him drink.
  Toronto mayor Allan Lamport

4. The penis is mightier than the sword.
  in a West Georgia Times *article*

5. It's not going to be peaches and gravy all the time.
  Pacers center Brad Miller, commenting on his team's struggles

6. Jihad is the knife slicing the salami of freedom.
  Danish "anti-Islamization" activist Anders Gravers Pedersen

7. The spectators are jumping around like dervishes at a teddy bears' picnic.
  radio broadcaster Ritchie Benaud

8. We just have to keep our heads to the grindstone and keep on grinding.
  Vikings quarterback Daunte Culpepper

9. Free societies will be allies against these hateful few who have no conscience, who kill at the whim of a hat.
  President George W. Bush

10. We'll cross that bridge when we fall off it.
  Canadian prime minister Lester Pearson

"We're Amazed These Haven't Happened Yet" Predictions

1. We stand on the threshold of rocket mail.

> *U.S. Postmaster General Arthur Summerfield, 1959*

2. Nuclear-powered vacuum cleaners will probably be a reality in ten years.

> *Alex Lewyt, president of vacuum cleaner company Lewyt Corp., in* The New York Times, *1955*

3. Human beings in the future will become one-toed. The small toes are being used less and less as time goes on, while the great toe is developing in an astonishing manner.

> *Richard Lucas, Royal College of Surgeons, 1911*

4. Brain work will cause her to become bald, while increasing masculinity and contempt for beauty will induce the growth of hair on her face. In the future, therefore, women will be bald and wear long mustaches and patriarchal beards.

> *Professor Hans Friedenthal of Berlin University, on the evolution of women after higher education and voting rights, 1914*

5. By 2000 . . . discarded paper table "linen" and rayon underwear will be bought by chemical factories and converted into candy.

> Science Digest, *1967*

6. Advertising will in the future become more and more intelligent in tone. It will seek to influence demand by argument instead of clamor. . . . Cheap attention-calling tricks will be wholly replaced, as they are already being replaced, by serious expression.

writer T. Baron Russell, in A Hundred Years Hence, *1905*

7. . . . computers in the future may have only 1,000 vacuum tubes and perhaps weigh only 1 H tons.

Popular Mechanics, *March 1949*

8. Peas and beans will be as large as beets are to-day. . . . Strawberries as large as apples will be eaten by our great-great-grandchildren for their Christmas dinners a hundred years hence. Raspberries and blackberries will be as large. One will suffice for the fruit course of each person.

John Elfreth Watkins Jr., in the Ladies' Home Journal, *1900*

9. There will be No C, X or Q in our every-day alphabet. They will be abandoned because unnecessary.

John Elfreth Watkins Jr., in the Ladies' Home Journal, *1900*

10. *The Life and Prophecies of Ursula Sontheil, 1881 edition:*

The world then to an end will come
In Eighteen Hundred and Eighty-one.

1882 edition:

The world then at an end we'll view
In Eighteen Hundred and Eighty-two

post-1882 editions:

The world then to an end will come
In Nineteen Hundred and Ninety One.

from a book supposedly written in 1488, later discovered to be the work of one Charles Hindley, a London bookseller

THE TOP 10 STUPIDEST
Amazingly Asinine Answers

1. So the obvious answer is Why?

> *newscaster John Humphrys*

2. **Food service manager:** Are you bilingual?

Job applicant (nervously): Well, um, yes, but only once in college.

> *during a job interview at a Minnesota casino*

3. **Beauty pageant judge:** Why do you think 1/5th of Americans can't locate the United States on a world map?

Miss South Carolina Teen Lauren Caitlin Upton: I personally believe that U.S. Americans are unable to do so because, um, some people out there in our nation don't have maps and, uh, I believe that our, uh, education like such as, uh, South Africa and, uh, the Iraq and everywhere like such as, and I believe that they should, uh, our education over here in the U.S. should help the U.S., uh, should help South Africa and should help Iraq and the Asian countries, so we will be able to build up our future.

4. **Q:** What does the thread count printed on the label of bed sheets and pillow cases indicate?

A: The massacre of Fort Mickinac in 1763 by Chief Pontiac of the Ottawas.

> Columbus (Ohio) Citizen

5. **Tech support:** How fast does your modem go?

Customer: It's not moving, it's just sitting there.

> *an actual computer tech-support call*

6. **Q:** What are the important safety tips to remember when backing your car?

A: Always wear a condom.

> *answer received on exams given by the California Department of Transportation's driving school*

7. **Reporter:** How do you feel about being named one of the NBA's most reporter-friendly players?

Basketball star Michael Jordan: No comment.

8. **Attorney:** Now, Mrs. Marsh, your complaint alleges that you have had problems with concentration since the accident. Does that condition continue today?

Plaintiff: No, not really. I take a stool softener now.

> *courtroom testimony*

9. **NBC newscaster John Chancellor:** How could you be sure the flying objects you saw were indeed UFOs?

Woman: They had the letters "UFO" on the side.

10. **Reporter:** Do the Broncos have your number, Christian?

Football player Christian Okoye: Do they have my number. I don't know. Do they have a guy with the number 35?

THE TOP 10 STUPIDEST
"I Wouldn't Want to Drink That Beverage" Names

1. Pee Cola
   soda, Ghana

2. California Pine Whizz
   soda, South Africa

3. Pipi
   orangeade, Yugoslavia

4. Kolic
   mineral water, Japan

5. Zit
   soft drink, Greece

6. Gag
   soft drink, France

7. Deepresso Coffee
   coffee drink, Japan

8. Libido
   soda, China

9. Hellena Fart
   fruit drink, Poland

10. Johnnie Worker Red Labial Old Scotch Whiskey
   whiskey, China

Things Ever Written or Said about Nuclear Stuff

1. *Nuclear War: What's in it for you?*
   book title

2. Nuclear weaponry, of course, would be the be-all, end-all of just too many people in too many parts of our planet.
   politician Sarah Palin, in a CBS interview with Katie Couric

3. The Atomic Energy Commission says the best defense against an atom bomb is to Be Somewhere Else when it bursts.
   in the civil defense film You & the Atom Bomb

4. Following a nuclear attack on the United States . . . every effort will be made to clear trans-nuclear checks, including those drawn on destroyed banks. You will be encouraged to buy US Savings Bonds.
   Federal Emergency Management Agency, Executive Order 11490

5. Brentwood Kelvedon Hatch
   Industrial Estates
   Secret Nuclear Bunker
   road sign, Essex, England

6. Area Man Wins Award for Nuclear Accident
   newspaper headline

7. [Nuclear war] is something that may not be desirable.

Attorney General Edwin Meese

8. ... many taxpayers will be inconvenienced by the hostilities [of thermonuclear war] and will have to be excused from paying the normal rate of interest on their debts.

IRS study

9. If a third or more of our population were killed in an atomic attack (a conservative estimate by the standards of the Rand Corporation's "Study of Nonmilitary Defense") a stronger estate tax would have a tremendous revenue potential.

from a 1963 Federal Reserve System planning document

10. Nuclear war could alleviate some of the factors leading to today's ecological disturbances that are due to current high-population concentrations and heavy industrial pollution.

Office of Civil Defense official, 1982

THE TOP 10 STUPIDEST
Lost in Translation
Moments

1. **Interviewer Mike Wallace (to Russian president Boris Yeltsin):** Are you thin-skinned about the press?

Translator (translating question into Russian): Are you a thick-skinned hippopotamus?

Russian president Boris Yeltsin: You should express yourself in a more civilized fashion!

2. **President Jimmy Carter:** I'm pleased to be here in Poland shaking your hands.

Polish translator: The president says he is pleased to be here in Poland grasping your private parts.

3. **German president Heinrich Lübke, on the tarmac in his role as official greeter in 1962, trying to say "how are you?":** Who are you?

President of India: I am the president of India.

4. **Chinese host, lifting his glass in a toast to his American guests:** Up your bottoms.

American diplomat: Up yours too.

> *overheard at a cocktail party boasting numerous international guests in Shenyang, China*

5. *Italian Government Biographies:*

- *Gianfranco Fini.* National Secretary of the Forehead of the Youth . . . expert of the Cones.
- *Rocco Buttiglione.* He has studied jurisprudence . . . under the guide of Prof. the Augosto of the Walnut
- *Umberto Bossi.* Been born, 1941. Conjugated, 4 sons. In 1979 enters into contact with the world and ne she becomes the flagman . . . Journalist, is founding of various various journalistic heads and average . . . he comes to an agreement himself with the Pole of Freedoms.

> *from the listing of government officials on the official website of the Italian government (www.governo.it), later removed*

6. **Translator:** Yes.
Lawyer: Yes?
Translator: Da?
Witness: Nyet.
Translator: No.
Lawyer: No?
Translator: Nyet?
Witness: Nyet.
Translator: No.

> *Raisa Korenblit, girlfriend of the slain Yakov Gluzman, at the trial of his wife, Rita Gluzman, being questioned by defense attorney Lawrence Hochheiser*

7. Australia and China are enjoying simultaneous orgasms in their relationship.

> *Australia's Labor Party leader Kevin Rudd, misinterpreting the Australian ambassador to China's speech in Mandarin Chinese*

8. Reporter (in German): How long has your team been training?

U.S. handball team coach Javier Cuesta (in English): We've been together since January, training five days a week, four to five hours a day.

Translator (taking microphone and also speaking English): We've been together since January, training five days a week, four to five hours a day.

> *during a press conference after a U.S.-Germany handball match*

9. When I look at my backside, I find it is divided into two parts.

> *Australian diplomat in France, trying to tell a French audience (in French) that, as he looked back over his career, it was divided into two units—before Paris and after Paris*

10. I will now open these trousers, and reveal some even more precious treasures to Your Royal Highness.

> *the archbishop of Uppsala, Sweden, trying to impress an English royal visitor with his knowledge of English*

Not-Terribly-Encouraging Advertising Claims

1. Suave Naturals Body Scrub

Costs less than more expensive brands.

label on Suave Naturals Body Scrub

2. Freshly ground coffee—Rich scent body odour genuine coffee flavour

menu item, China

3. Order anything on our menu and

We'll Step on It!

ad for the Midwestern chain Green Mill Restaurant & Bar

4. Makes walking tiring.

slogan on shoes in Jakarta

5. Jumping Vitamins: You can't keep them down!

     slogan for Indian medication

6. Everyday High Price!

     sign in a store window, Tokyo, Japan

7. Today's feature: Apples the size of garbanzo beans

     sign outside of Jim's Fruit and Produce, Belle Plaine, Minnesota

8. Vintage English Man's Grooming Brush with
Come on Top!

     *eBay auction listing (which was supposed to say
"comb on top")*

9. Le Cafe—Arcadia Hotel: You have no reason to try our
restaurant.

     slogan on a menu at Le Cafe in the Arcadia Hotel, Jakarta

10. Swagger body wash from Old Spice is for the man who
holds the complete works of Aristotle in one hand, and
a delicious sandwich in the other.

     the back of a bottle of Old Spice Swagger Body Wash

THE TOP 10 STUPIDEST

Truly Toxic
Environment Enunciations

1. It isn't pollution that's harming our environment. It's the impurities in our air and water that are doing it.

> *Vice President Dan Quayle*

2. Clean water is one of the leading causes of death in the world.

> *singer Jewel, trying to explain the need for better water filtration systems*

3. We were trying to show that Earth First! isn't a fringe element. We had pretty impressive individuals [at the protest]. We had people who run companies. We had clergy. We had a Jewish rabbi. Well, he's not a rabbi, but he's a Jewish optometrist.

> *Sig-Britt Cox, protest organizer for the environmental activist group Earth First!, talking about an anti-logging protest*

4. *How Green Were the Nazis?*

> *book title*

5. Mr. Friendly Quality Eraser. Mr Friendly Arrived! He always stay near you and steals in your mind to lead you to a good situation. We are ecologically minded. This package will self-destruct in Mother Earth.

> *on a Japanese eraser*

6. The government is not doing enough about cleaning up the environment. This is a great planet.

contestant for Mr. New Jersey Male, when asked what he would do with a million dollars

7. You talk about the environment—take a look at the Arkansas River. And I'll have more to say about that in a minute. We've even seen some chickens along the way. Here's one back here. But I can't figure that out or maybe he's talking about the Arkansas River again where they're dumping that—I've got to be careful here—that fecal—some kind of bacteria into the river. Too much from the chicken.

President George H. W. Bush

8. I applaud the people that are trying to save species that are endangered, but it might be good that we don't have dinosaurs now. We've gotten oil from dinosaurs. If we had preserved the dinosaur, we wouldn't have that oil.

Washington Association of Wheat Growers lobbyist Gretchen Borck

9. Too many bugs and leeches and spiders and spider webs. Please spray the wilderness to rid the area of these pests.

comments made to Forest Service by hikers completing wilderness camping trips

10. The coyotes made too much noise last night and kept me awake. Please eradicate these annoying animals.

comments made to Forest Service by hikers completing wilderness camping trips

Income Tax–Related Inanities

1. You will find it a distinct help . . . if you know and look as if you know what you are doing.

IRS training manual for tax auditors

2. Definition of a qualifying child revised. The following changes to the definition of a qualifying child have been made: Your qualifying child must be younger than you.

from Publication 919 Cat. No. 63900P of the IRS, "How Do I Adjust My Tax Withholding," Page 2

3. I want to be sure [the new IRS commissioner] is a ruthless son of a bitch, that he will do what he's told, that every income-tax return I want to see I see, that he will go after our enemies and not our friends. Now, it's as simple as that. If he isn't, he doesn't get the job.

President Richard Nixon, in May 1971 tapes

4. This information is being furnished to the Infernal Revenue Service.

printed on a tax form 1099-R, Sacramento, California

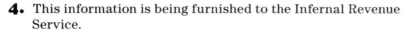

5. For purposes of paragraph (3), an organization described in paragraph (2) shall be deemed to include an organization described in section 501(c)(4), (5) or (6) which would be described in paragraph (2) if it were an organization described in section 501(c)(3).

section of the Internal Revenue Code

6. I want to find out who this FICA guy is and how come he's taking so much of my money.

hockey player Nick Kypreos, explaining what he planned to do during his Stanley Cup winning team's visit to the White House

7. Illegal income, such as stolen or embezzled money, must be included in your gross income.

helpful information posted on the official Internal Revenue Service website

8. During state of national emergency resulting from enemy attack, the essential functions of the Internal Revenue Service will be as follows: (1) assessing, collecting, and recording taxes. . . .

Internal Revenue Service Handbook

9. Passive activity income does not include the following: Income for an activity that is not a passive activity.

IRS Form 8583, Passive Activity Loss Limitation

10. Like, a lot of us are making a lot of money now, and so we're paying a lot of taxes, you know. Is there, like, a way I can just write on the memo line of my check what I want my taxes to go for, like for school?

actress Justine Bateman, at a lecture given by Sen. John Kerry (D-Massachusetts)

Purely Accidental Poop References

1. Jeans: Low-rise Styles Continue to be Poopular among Young Adults

> *headline,* Las Vegas Review-Journal

2. JENSEN'S COUNTRY FOODS OLD TIME BAKERY

Sesame or Poopy Seed French Bread

> *ad for a market and bakery, Palm Springs, California*

3. Chicken Poopy lip balm $3.99

> *sign in a Walgreen's window, Indianapolis*

4. And now, his poopiness the Hole . . . er . . . His poopiness the Pole . . . rather, His Holiness the Poop.

> *translator at a meeting in the Vatican*

5. Rice Pooping

> *dessert offered on a Japanese menu*

6. Nokia
connocting poopie
store sign, Japan

7. Opium Poopy Production Talks
headline on a French news site

8. Poop Beauty Shop
beauty salon, Aichi, Japan

9. *Mr. Cat Poop*
title of the film As Good as It Gets, *as released in Hong Kong*

10. Poop-Fried Pork with Onion
menu item, Singapore

A-Little-Too-Creative Imagery-Rich Statements from Sportscasters

1. [There's] bound to be a deeply beating heart inside that young brain.
sportscaster Bill Leslie

2. He plucked the ball out of the air like a salmon.
sportscaster Ray French

3. Neil Baker is standing on the touchline with his hands in his tracksuit bottoms scratching his head.
sportscaster Chris Kamara

4. The goalkeeper—his left hand just disintegrated!
sportscaster Peter Beagrie

5. Luis Tiant comes from everywhere except between his legs.
sportscaster Curt Gowdy

6. Watch the expression on his mask.
hockey sportscaster Harry Neale

7. People will look at Bowyer and Woodgate and say "Well, there's no mud without flames."

sportscaster Gordon Taylor

8. A smoked salmon sandwich of a football match if ever there has been one.

sportscaster Peter Drury

9. They've picked their heads up off the ground and they now have a lot to carry on their shoulders.

sportscaster Ron Atkinson

10. Many different kinds of animals have interrupted football games, but perhaps none so unusual as this one: "It's a big, Hippity-hop rabbit, jacking off down the field."

sportscaster

Technically Correct but Not Quite Right Game Show Answers

1. *Family Feud* **host Richard Karn:** Name a sport husbands and wives can play together.

Contestant: Kickball.

2. *Family Fortunes* **host:** We asked a hundred people to name a place where you wouldn't expect to meet a nun.

Female contestant: A brothel.

3. *Family Fortunes* **host:** Name the capital of France.

Contestant: F.

4. *Family Feud* **host Richard Dawson:** Something Russia's famous for.

Contestant: Russians.

5. *Family Fortunes* **host:** Name something that flies that doesn't have an engine?

Contestant: A bicycle with wings.

6. *Family Feud* **host Richard Dawson:** Name something that gets wet when you use it.
Contestant: Toilet paper.

7. *Family Fortunes* **host:** Name something made of wool.
Contestant: Sheep.

8. **Game show host:** What does Dad traditionally do after dinner on Thanksgiving?
Young contestant: Poop.

9. *Family Fortunes* **host:** We surveyed a hundred people and asked them to name a way of toasting someone. Michelle?
Contestant: Over a fire.

10. *Family Fortunes* **host:** We asked a hundred people what a girl should know about a man before she marries him. Lynn, what would you say?
Contestant: His name.

"Except for" Qualifications

1. Other than being castrated, things have gone quite well for Funny Cide.

> *ESPN sports analyst Kenny Mayne, about the horse Funny Cide*

2. I robbed from the rich, kind of like Robin Hood, except I kept it.

> *convicted thief Bill Becker*

3. I didn't think there were too many problems other than two interceptions in the red zone and one blocked field goal.

> *football player Steven Young, after a losing game*

4. I'm playing as well as I've ever played, except for the years I played better.

> *golfer Fred Couples*

5. Full disclosure is the worst we can do, except for everything else.

> *chief technology officer of an Internet security company, commenting on his company's strategy*

6. The lead car is absolutely unique, except for the one behind it
which is identical.

> *racing commentator Murray Walker*

7. I could have been a Rhodes Scholar, except for my grades.

> *Michigan State football coach Duffy Daugherty*

8. If you set aside Three Mile Island and Chernobyl, the safety record
of nuclear is really very good.

> *Treasury Secretary Paul O'Neill, explaining the Bush administration's
> advocacy of nuclear power*

9. Our Cabinet is always unanimous, except when we disagree.

> *premier of British Columbia, Canada, Bill Vander Zalm*

10. In a sense it's a one-man show . . . except there are two men involved,
Hartson and Berkovic, and a third man, the goal keeper.

> *sportscaster John Motson*

Historically Dubious Moments in Film

1. Oh, Moses, Moses, you stubborn, splendid, adorable fool!
>   *Nefretiri to Moses, in* The Ten Commandments *(1956)*

2. Romulus Augustus: Mother, am I now the most powerful man in the world?

Flavia: Of course you are.

Romulus Augustus: Then why can't I stay out tonight?
>   The Last Legion *(2007)*

3. Michelangelo, make up your mind, once and for all: do you want to finish that ceiling?
>   *question posed to the artist, in*
>   The Agony and the Ecstasy *(1965)*

4. My breasts are full of love and life. My hips are round and well apart. Such women, they say, have sons.
>   *Cleopatra seducing Caesar,*
>   *in* Cleopatra *(1963)*

5. Bortai (trying to kill Genghis Khan): For me, there is no peace while you live, Mongol!

Genghis Khan: You're beautiful in your wrath!
>   The Conqueror *(1956)*

6. It's not just about how far we've come, it's this bitch of a wind.

the captain of the Pinta *to Columbus, in* Christopher Columbus: The Discovery *(1992)*

7. War! War! That's all you think of, Dick Plantagenet! You burner! You pillager!

Lady Edith, in King Richard and the Crusaders *(1954)*

8. You mean I'm gonna get *paid* to play baseball? Boy, a hundred dollars! There's not that much money in the whole world!

young Babe Ruth, in The Babe Ruth Story *(1948)*

9. Don't shout, I'm not deaf!

composer Ludwig von Beethoven, in The Melody Master *(1941)*

Huh?

Beethoven proving that he is *deaf, in* The Melody Master

10. Unless I miss my guess, we're in for one wild night.

King Leonidas, in 300 *(2006)*

THE TOP 10 STUPIDEST

Not-Very-Helpful Examples from "Teach Yourself English" Phrase Books

1. *Can't You Speak English? Yes, I Am!*
       title of an English language book, Korea

2. I'm verry sorry I clogged the sink. I just didn't want to vomit on the floor.
       sentence #12 in the Japanese book Making Excuses in English

3. At the Fruit Shop:

"Hello, fruiterer! Have you some nice fruits here? How much for a bench of bananas?

"Five hundreds rupiahs."

"The price is okay. Give me two benches please. Thank you. I hope I don't bore to come here again."
       suggested conversation in the book English Conversations, *Indonesia*

4. Fancy giving free education! This is a paradise for the people, indeed!

His Excellency Kim Il Sung is the greatest genius of the present times.

Here is a bumper crop. We have a bumper crop every year.

Bookseller! Have you "Kim Il Sung Selected Works" Vol 1,2,3,4,5,6?
       some suggested catchy phrases to learn in the North Korean government book Speak in Korean

5. To use an English phrase, he is a host in himself.
       from the English-Chinese Word Ocean Dictionary

6. The human being today is undergoing suffering of different kinds. On the one hand there is poverty and hunger. On the other hand developed societies are yearning for dinner peace.

> *from the* Bangkok Post *website: "Learing English with the Post"*

7. Bring me a partion of . . .

Only a half a partion of . . .

Smocking/No Smocking

Bring me, we are in a harry!

This is to go at deffered rate (halt rate)

I cannot speek . . .

> *"helpful words and phrases" listed in* Learn Greek with Me,
> English-Greek Dictionary, *Athens, 1982*

8. Just remember this acronym—DOSSiShQACNMN—to make it easy for you to remember the order of adjectives in a series.

> *in an English language learning book used in the Philippines*

9. To craunch a marmoset.

Do you cut the hairs?

The stone as roll not heap up not foam.

Nothing some money, nothing of Swiss.

Exculpate me by your brother's

> *catchy English phrases to learn in* The New Guide of the Conversation in Portuguese and English, *written by Pedro Carolino in 1883*

10. You've mistaken that banana for a telephone!

> *handy English phrase in a Japanese textbook*

Deeply Moronic Insights from Deeply Concerned Celebrities

1. I think it is really important people eat.

actress Tara Reid, after learning what the 50th annual Citymeals-on-Wheels lunch was for

2. I want to be like Gandhi and Martin Luther King and John Lennon, but I want to stay alive.

singer Madonna

3. It's important to be thankful, even if you're poor. I mean, come on, we all have clean water—well, OK, not people in the developing world.

singer Avril Lavigne

4. No, I think I'm sassy. But my parents taught me to be a very kind person, to be compassionate . . . At Spence, one of my friends was a girl who was handicapped. And I have a friend who had a craniofacial deformity. That's not something that frightens me. So, I'm sassy.

actress/singer Emmy Rossum

5. I knocked someone over in Mombasa and he broke his leg. But I gave him £10 and he seemed really pleased.

model Caprice

6. I look at [modeling] as something I'm doing for black people in general.

model Naomi Campbell

7. I don't go tanning anymore because Obama put a 10% tax on tanning. I feel like he did that intentionally for us, like McCain would never put a 10% tax on tanning . . . because he is pale and he would probably wanna be tanned.

Jersey Shore *reality star Snooki*

8. Beyond its entertainment value, *Baywatch* has enriched and, in many cases, helped save lives.

actor David Hasselhoff

9. [Starring as Joan of Arc] was incredibly trying on a physical level, but what kept me going was the thought that no matter how difficult it was for me, I knew it had been a lifetime more difficult for Joan.

actress Milla Jovovich, commenting on her role as Joan of Arc—who was burned at the stake

10. Most people aren't pooing. I know two girls in my life who are good friends, who were not pooing, but now they're pooing 'cause I helped them. I taught them how to poo.

actress Alicia Silverstone

"Gee, We Didn't Know *That*" Statements

1. If you throw at someone's head, it's very dangerous, because in the head is the brain.

> *baseball player Ivan "Pudge" Rodriguez*

2. Research by the U.S. Navy has determined that water freezes in cold weather.

> *first line of an article in a Southfield, Michigan, newspaper*

3. As the ball gets softer it loses its hardness.

> *sportscaster Geoff Boycott*

4. If you are an airman, then you believe that airpower, if used in certain ways, will achieve victory more quickly than if used in other ways.

> *from a U.S. Air Force ROTC presentation on the University of California, Berkeley, website*

5. If you make the right decision, it's normally going to be the correct one.

> *soccer player Dave Beasant*

6. [I]t's the millennium Wimbledon. There won't be another millennium Wimbledon for another millennium.

> *tennis star Venus Williams*

7. Warning—If doubling ingredients you will make twice as many.

> *printed after a recipe in a Sainsbury's cooking magazine*

8. As soon as you see it— it's visible.

> *closet organizer Linda Cohen*

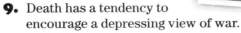

9. Death has a tendency to encourage a depressing view of war.

> *Secretary of Defense Donald Rumsfeld*

10. The painting, *Wheatfield with Crows*, probably painted before Van Gogh committed suicide.

> *caption under photo of Van Gogh's famous painting, in* Malay Mail *(Malaysia)*

THE TOP 10 STUPIDEST
Christmas Stupidities

1. "Perry Como's Christmas Special": The members of Greek family are murdered systematically in a bizarre fashion.

> Toronto (Ontario) Sun *television page listing*

2. A holy symbol like Frosty (the Snowman) should not be taken away from Christmas. Well, maybe that is a bad example.

> Fox & Friends *anchor Brian Kilmeade, discussing the secularization of Christmas*

3. For your shopping convenience, we will be closed Christmas Day.

> *sign on door of a Boston supermarket*

4. Christmas Sale of Methodist Women at West-Side Church

> Springfield (Massachusetts) Daily News

5. And there you can see the official state Christmas tree on the lawn of the State House. And, right next to it, you can see the state Christmas menorah.

> *on a Boston nightly news show*

6. Call Wieser's for Home Made Fruit Cake: Solid Mahogany.

> The Free Lance-Star
> *(Fredericksburg, Virginia)*

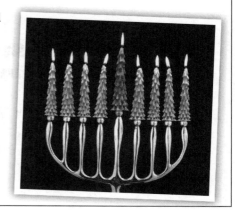

7. **Q:** What would you like most for Christmas? (asked in 1948 by a Washington radio station of different ambassadors in D.C.):

French ambassador: Peace throughout the world.

Soviet ambassador: Freedom for all people enslaved by imperialism.

British ambassador Sir Oliver Franks: Well, it's very kind of you to ask. I'd quite like a box of crystallized fruit.

8. On December 5th, come in with your friends and family and paint your balls for Christmas.

sign in an Atlanta, Georgia, restaurant

9. Christmas Fun Special
Good Sense
Hemmorhoidal Suppositories
24 count/$6.99

in a drugstore flyer

10. If you wish hard enough, your Christmas dearms really will come ture.

Christmas card, China

. . . And the 10 Stupidest Christmas Carols, Hymns, and Oratory

1. Our next song will be "Angels We Have Heard Get High."

in a church bulletin

2. We now will hear Deck Your Balls with Halls of Helly . . . Deck Your Bells with Balls of Holly . . . er . . . a Christmas selection.

BBC radio announcer

3. Gracious God, we are saturated with Christmas celebrating: the shopping, the merry mating. . . .

in a church bulletin

4. Hark the Harold Angel

Christmas carol listed in a Bangkok church bulletin

5. Mary was that mother mild,
Jesus Christ, her little Chili.

printing of the text of the Christmas carol "Once in Royal David's City," in a church Christmas bulletin

6. Look now for glad and golden hours come swiftly on the wing
O rest beside the weary toad and hear the angels sing

lyrics for "It Came Upon the Midnight Clear," as printed in a brochure for a Redmond, Washington, church

7. He's making a list
And checking it twice
Gonna find out
Who's knotty and nice

"Santa Claus Is Comin' to Town" lyrics printed on SongLyrics.com

8. Oh Little Toe of Bethlehem how still we see thee lie.

in a church Christmas bulletin

9. Silent night! Holy night!
Son of God, love's pure light
Radiant beans from Thy Holy Face

lyrics printed in a church bulletin

10. I Saw Murray Kissing Santa Claus

Kowloon (Hong Kong) school handout

And Least Confidence-Building Business, Etc., Names

1. Slasher Barber and Massage Center
barber shop, Philippines

2. Very Suspicious Supermarket
supermarket, Taiwan

3. The Overcoming Faith Ministries
sign on church outside Robertsdale, Alabama

4. Titanic Tours & Travel
travel agency, Udaipur, Rajasthan, India

5. Oily Beauty Centre
beauty salon, Hong Kong

6. Pub Hangover
bar, Tel Aviv, Israel

7. Neo Nazi Service
video store, Nonthaburi (suburb of Bangkok), Thailand

8. UglyGirl Boutique
fashion boutique, Beijing, China

9. Greasy Fast Food Restaurant
restaurant, Quezon City, Philippines

10. Dead Fish Restaurant
Siem Reap, Cambodia

Moments in Press Conferences

1. **Lena Guerrero, first female Texas railroad commissioner, addressing a group of truckers:** Does anyone have any questions?

Audience member: What is your bra size?

2. That's a good question and let me state the problem more clearly without going too deeply into the answer.
> *National Security Advisor Brent Scowcroft, at a press briefing*

3. First of all, I don't think I called for a deadline. I thought I said, time—I did? What exactly did I say? I said, "deadline"? Okay, yes, then I meant what I said.
> *President George W. Bush, at a press conference in Albania*

4. **Reporter:** Were the White House coffee meetings with wealthy donors used for fund-raising?

Clinton press seccretary Mike McCurry: Technically, they were not used for fund-raising, but they became an element of the financial program that we were trying to pursue in connection with the campaign.

5. As I said already, they have conducted themselves in the last two or three years, much more discri—er, discree—discri—uh, with greater prudence and discretion that we have because it is, uh, I—I've forgotten what the question was.
> *Sen. J. William Fulbright (D-Arkansas) during a press conference, trying to smoothly answer a reporter's question*

6. **Reporter:** How many NATO strikes have been aborted due to bad weather?

Vice Admiral Scott Fry: I'm afraid I can't get into that level of detail right off the top of my head.

Reporter: How about an approximation?

Fry: I'd prefer not to even approximate it.

Reporter: How about a ballpark figure?

Fry: I don't have that information available.

Reporter: How many of [Yugoslavian Premier] Milošević's surface to air missle launchers have been taken out by NATO?

Fry: That's a military number I'm not going to talk about.

Reporter: How about a guess?

Fry: A large percentage.

Reporter: A large percentage of the missle launchers?

Fry: The launchers themselves, no.

> *Pentagon briefing on the Kosovo war*

7. **Reporter:** Mr. Secretary, has anyone asked you the whereabouts of Mr. Molotov?

Secretary of State Dean Rusk (just back from a Moscow summit): No. No one has asked me that question. You can if you want to.

Reporter: Well, sir, where is Mr. Molotov?

Rusk: I haven't the faintest idea.

8. Some of our friends are for it. Some of our friends are against it. And we're standing with our friends.

> *White House press secretary Mike McCurry, explaining whether or not President Clinton would veto a bill curbing securities lawsuits*

9. **Reporter:** Do you know to what extent the U.S. and Colombia are in fact cooperating militarily now, in terms of interdiction efforts?

President George H. W. Bush: Well, I—Yes, I know that.

Reporter: Can you share that with us?

Bush: No.

Reporter: Why not, sir?

Bush: Because I don't feel like it.

at a press conference just before Bush was going to attend a drug summit in Colombia

10. I would feel that most of the conversations that took place in those areas of the White House that did have the recording system would in almost their entirety be in existence but the special prosecutor, the court, and, I think, the American people are sufficiently familiar with the recording system to know where the recording devices existed and to know the situation in terms of the recording process but I feel, although the process has not been undertaken yet in preparation of the material to abide by the court decision, really, what the answer to that question is.

Nixon press secretary Ron Ziegler

Bad Calls

1. I'd rather be dead than singing "Satisfaction" when I'm forty-five.

rocker Mick Jagger, before he hit 45

2. With over 50 cars already on sale here, the Japanese auto industry isn't likely to carve out a big slice of the U.S. market for itself.

commentary in Business Week *magazine, 1968*

3. I'm going to be bigger than the Beatles.

Irish singer Crispian St. Peters, after his 1966 hit "You Were on My Mind"

4. I see no good reasons why the views given in this volume should shock the religious sensibilities of anyone.

Charles Darwin, in The Origin Of Species, *1869*

5. Google's not a real company. It's a house of cards.

Microsoft CEO Steve Ballmer, in a court transcript

6. There's no chance that the iPhone is going to get any significant market share. No chance.

Microsoft CEO Steve Ballmer

7. Rembrandt is not to be compared in the painting of character with our extraordinarily gifted English artist, Mr. Rippingille.

British art critic and scholar John Hunt

8. Space travel is utter bilge.

Sir Richard Woolley, 1950s astronomer royal of Britain

9. Radio has no future.

Lord Kelvin, president of the Royal Society and disbeliever in virtually every scientific discovery

10. You'll never make it. . . . Go back to Liverpool.

Decca Records executive, to the Beatles in 1962

Most Incredibly Annoying Things Said by Rich People

1. It's so bad being homeless in winter. They should go somewhere warm like the Caribbean where they can eat fresh fish all day.

model/socialite Lady Victoria Hervey

2. I always lived very frugally. I flew around on a private jet. I had a boat. But I always lived very frugally.

billionaire financier and alleged Ponzi scheme operator Allen Stanford

3. What was hard [during this recession] was giving up my live-in maid five days a week. My daughter said, do we really need somebody? So I cut back, and I just hired somebody for two days. And you know, it kind of brought our family together. We cook together more as a family. Normally when the housekeeper was there cooking for us, my husband would be off with the paper and I would be on the phone with my friends and the kids were doing homework. I do have the woman make one extra dinner for us though, and one or two nights we do order in, and a lot of times we will go out.

Real Housewives of New York City *star Ramona Singer*

4. I have not been to my house in Bermuda for two or three years—and the same goes for my house in Portofino. . . . How long do I have to keep leading this life of sacrifice?

Italian prime minister Silvio Berlusconi

5. [I'm] insulted by the offer of $10 million per year. I've got my family to feed.

basketball player Latrell Sprewell

6. It's the summer season coming up, so my patients must have [plastic surgery] tuneups. But instead of doing liposuction on seven areas, they're doing three or four. These decisions are so painful.

plastic surgeon Pamela Lipkin, explaining the difficulties of the economic downturn

7. I can't understand all the fuss about student grants. Carol managed to save out of hers. Of course, we paid for her skiing holidays.

British prime minister Margaret Thatcher, talking about how easy it is to save for college

8. Don Simpson had no money. Maybe $30 million at the most. That's nothing.

producer Jon Peters

9. **Q:** What are you getting paid to direct and star in this film?
Barbra Streisand: I'd rather not talk about money. It's kind of gross.

10. There's no way to make everybody rich. I don't even know if it's worth the trouble because the life of a rich person, in general, is very boring.

Brazilian president Fernando Henrique Cardoso

Things Said about Death, Suicide, Murder, and Other Light Topics

1. I had thought very carefully about committing hara-kiri (ritual suicide) over this, but I overslept this morning.

> *former Japanese labor minister Toshio Yamaguchi, after being arrested*

2. Smoking kills. If you're killed, you've lost a very important part of your life.

> *actress Brooke Shields, when testifying to Congress*

3. As yet there has been no reaction from the man who was murdered.

> *newscaster, BBC News*

4. Man Thought Hurt but Slightly Dead

> *headline,* The Providence (Rhode Island) Journal

5. The only way to stop this suicide wave is to make it a capital offense, punishable by death.

> *Irish member of Parliament during a debate*

6. It is thought that Raj Mohammed Poselay was beaten to death, possibly during a family fun day in the park.

Woleverhampton (UK) Express & Star

7. Keep chair on position and table cleaned after dying. Thank you for your corporation.

sign in a restaurant, Japan

8. We were disturbed by the ridicule because death, especially to the person who has just experienced it, is not funny.

spokesman for a national funeral director's association

9. Health department says death certificates are to be ordered one week in advance of death

Lancaster (Ohio) Eagle-Gazette

10. Please tell the public not to kill themselves on hotel property if they want to die. It only confounds us. They can do it in the river for example.

assistant public relations manager of the Jakarta Hilton, after a death at the hotel, as reported in The Jakarta (Indonesia) Post

THE TOP 10 STUPIDEST
Over-the-Top
Rants and Raves

1. Down with the greedy Stamp Bourgeoisie! Long Live the Red
Philatelic International, leader and guardian of the world's working
class philatelists and numismatists! Proletarian stamp and coin
collectors, Unite!

> *from the front page of the 1924 Russian magazine for stamp collectors,*
> Red Philatelist

2. No! No! I don't want cheese! I can't see cheese! I can't eat cheese!
I'm allergic to cheese!

> *televangelist Rev. Robert Schuller, who got upset when an airline*
> *flight attendant tried to serve him cheese.*
> *Schuller then reportedly*
> *demanded all the grapes*
> *on the flight instead*
> *of cheese.*

3. I thought it was an
amazing script. Just in
terms of narrative, man,
there's cows, bang! bang!
bang!, porno shops,
salmon swimming, blow
jobs, money-exchanging,
and then I burst in Idaho,
smash!

> *actor Keanu Reeves*

4. They use their color blind the way duck hunters use their duck blind! They hide behind the phrase and just hope that we, like the ducks, won't be able to see through it. . . . The Gospel of Luke tells us of Jesus' reaction to people who willfully refused to see the evidence before their eyes. . . . Ye Hypocrites!!

   Vice President Al Gore

5. [R]ight now all of us together, all of us together would go down to Washington and we should stone Henry Hyde to death! Wait! Shut up! Shut up! No, shut up! I'm not finished. We would stone Henry Hyde to death and would go to their homes and we'd kill their wives and children. We would kill their families!

   actor and political aspirant Alec Baldwin, on the Conan O'Brien show

6. Scenes that will stagger your sight!

Dancing called go-go

- Music called ju-ju
- Narcotics called bang!
- Fires of puberty!

See the burning of a virgin!

See power of witch doctor over women!

See pygmies with fantastic Physical Endowments!!!

   ad for the film Kwaheri *(1964)*

7. How dare you fold the towels in the room like that! That's not how I fold them at home! I reserved this room a month ago, you knew I was coming here!

   comment made to a front desk employee of a major hotel

8. God, I'm hot from that tea! Woo! All the sudden, I'm like, woo, warm! That actually happens to me if I have a hot drink! Yeah, yeah!

> *actress Kate Bosworth*

9. Noooooo coooooookies!!! No f∗∗∗ing cookies! I have guests who want cookies! Just what do you expect me to tell them! You f∗∗∗ing fool! No cookies because you didn't bother to check! And you're supposed to be in charge! You go and tell my guests that you are so stupid you forgot the cookies!

> *actress Marlo Thomas to her butler during a luncheon she gave for Gloria Steinem (as reported in* That Girl and Phil *by Desmond Atholl)*

10. How dare you serve cold cuts in my house. It's just so low class and common. And white bread and pickles! And my God, *meat* lasagna!!! F∗∗∗er, you've done it again.

> *actress Marlo Thomas still talking to her butler (as reported in* That Girl and Phil *by Desmond Atholl)*

Stupidest-Sounding Scientific Studies

1. Chickens Prefer Beautiful Humans

2. The Significance of Mr. Richard Buckley's Exploding Trousers

3. An Analysis of the Forces Required to Drag Sheep Over Various Surfaces

4. Effects of Backward Speech and Speaker Variability in Language Discrimination by Rats

5. Fellatio by Fruit Bats Prolongs Copulation Time

6. Microbial Treatment of Kitchen Refuse with Enzyme-Producing Thermophilic Bacteria from Giant Panda Feces

7. Spontaneous Knotting of an Agitated String

8. Will Humans Swim Faster or Slower in Syrup?

9. On the Comparative Palatability of Some Dry-Season Tadpoles from Costa Rica

10. Impact of Wet Underwear on Thermoregulatory Responses and Thermal Comfort in the Cold

Say What? Moments

1. I hope you believe you understand what you think I said, but I'm not sure you realize that what you've heard is not what I meant.

   President Richard Nixon

2. A proof is a proof. What kind of a proof? It's a proof. A proof is a proof and when you have a good proof is because it's proven.

   Canadian prime minister Jean Chrétien

3. He's got a heart as big as his size, which isn't big—but his heart's bigger than that.

   soccer manager Kevin Keegan

4. These items may or may not be available at all times, and sometimes not at all and other times all the time.

   menu at a Fort Bragg, California, restaurant

5. There are known knowns. There are things we know that we know. We also know there are known unknowns. That is to say, we know there are some things we don't know. But there are also unknown unknowns— the ones we don't know we don't know.

   Defense Secretary Donald Rumsfeld, author of the memoir Known and Unknown

6. Tonight he became the name we've all been hoping he'd become—the man, in fact, that he has been for some time now.

soccer manager Martin O'Neill

7. I never say what I mean, but I always manage to say something similar.

conductor Eugene Ormandy

8. The film had the third best Wednesday ever and the seventh best Wednesday of all time.

radio newscaster, Arizona

9. Yeah, you'd have to be disappointed not to be pleased.

rugby coach Michael Hagan

10. When you take a portion of an interview out of context, or a portion of a context of an interview, you run the risk of actually not getting the entire context of that particular interview.

British Columbia minister of housing and social development Rich Coleman

Yet Strangely Fascinating Lines from News Stories

1. Earlier today, Hillary Clinton was launched on a cruise missile.

closed caption, Detroit-area newscast

2. Sir Hugh and Lady Carlton received many congratulations after their horse's success. The latter wore a yellow frock trimmed with picot-edge frills and a close-fitting hat.

Berkshire (UK) newspaper

3. It's been a long time since I caught crabs. The last occasion was 15 years ago on the Isle of Wight. Oh, what a long, hot summer that was.

journalist Bryony Gordon, in a Daily Telegraph *(UK) story*

4. Lambert said the suspects wore socks on their heads, probably to keep from leaving any fingerprints.

newspaper in Mount Sterling, Kentucky

5. The pilot of the fighter, identified as Captain Kin Young-bae, was reported to have ejaculated shortly before the crash to safety and was evacuated to a nearby military hospital.

Korea Times

6. He also said an older woman suffered a broken hip when a dog pounced on her and read a long letter from someone supporting the dog ban.

Tybee (Tybee Island, Georgia) News

7. [Candidate Edward D. Kusta Jr.] and his wife, Nicole, have a bulldog named Jekyll. He holds a bachelor's degree in business from Northern Illinois University and a juris doctorate from Thomas M. Cooley Law School.

newspaper in Illinois

8. Among the various tourism arrangements, the technology tour is perhaps the most unusual, taking travelers to places where earlier foreign visitors would have been most unwelcome and possibly branded as "spices."

China Travel *magazine*

9. Edward Montagu's is an unconventional life story. Born in 1926, he succeeded to the peerage in 1929 having been educated at Eton and New College, Oxford.

The Daily Telegraph *(UK)*

10. Mrs. Lea made no mention of the nationality of the kidnappers nor gave details of her husband's discovery, but he was apparently kept in a darkened hut for two days. He had been roughed up and beaten by insects, the police said.

The Evening News *(UK)*

Things to Say to an Alien (According to Dreadful Science Fiction Films)

1. **Col. Edwards:** Why is it so important that you want to contact the governments of our Earth?

Eros the alien: Because of death. *Because all of you of Earth are idiots!*

Fighter pilot: Now you just hold on, buster!

> *Tom Keene (the colonel), Dudley Manlove (the alien), and Gregory Walcott (the pilot), in* Plan 9 from Outer Space *(1959)*

2. **Alien:** It should interest you to know that I have visited hundreds of other worlds and your Earth seems most suitable.

Submarine commander: Swell!

> *Bug-eyed alien and Earth fellow having a conversation, in* The Atomic Submarine *(1960)*

3. **Billy:** Who are you?

Kimar: We're from Mars. Don't be afraid, we have children just like you on Mars.

Betty: What are those funny things sticking out of your head?

Kimar: Those are our antennae.

Betty: Are you a television set?

> *Earth children meet the Martians, in* Santa Claus Conquers the Martians *(1964)*

4. **Moon maiden:** Do you have rock creatures on Earth?

Teenage astronaut: No. And if I was out with a pretty girl on Earth, I wouldn't be talking about them either!

> *Love-struck space duo, in* Missile to the Moon *(1958)*

5. Can we talk this over? It looks like you're going to sing "White Christmas." . . . You've broken my mind!

> *Christopher Walken, as novelist and alien abductee popularizer Whitley Strieber, talking to bug-eyed aliens, in* Communion *(1989)*

6. **Earthman (in a very bad spacesuit, talking to a nude moon woman):** Hello. I saw you on the throne before. You must be the queen. I've brought something for you. On Earth we call this candy.

[Gives her some candy in wax paper. She spits out the candy and eats the wrapper.]

Earthman: Ha, ha—ha, ha—ho, ho—You're not supposed to eat the paper.

> *in* Nude on the Moon *(1961)*

7. Eros the alien: Your scientists stumbled upon the atom bomb—split the atom! Then the hydrogen bomb, where you actually explode the air itself. Now you bring the total destruction of the entire universe, served by our sun. The only explosion left is the solaronite.

Fighter pilot: So what if we do develop this solaronite bomb— we'd be even a stronger nation than now!

Eros the alien: Stronger? You see! You see! Your stupid minds! Stupid! Stupid!

Fighter pilot: That's all I'm taking from you! [He punches the alien.]

> *Dudley Manlove (the alien) and Gregory Walcott (the pilot),*
> *in* Plan 9 from Outer Space *(1959)*

8. Wow! That's the first time a salad's ever tossed me!

> *American G.I. (Bob Ball) after a fight with an alien giant carrot, in*
> Invasion of the Star Creatures *(1962)*

9. 1st astronaut: Why, it's a woman!

2nd astronaut: You can say that again—with all the necessary ingredients!

> *two astonished astronauts meeting a woman on the 13th moon of*
> *Jupiter, in* Fire Maidens of Outer Space *(1956)*

10. Twenty-six million miles from Earth and the dolls are just the same.

> *flight crew member, in* Queen of Outer Space *(1958)*

Meteorological Misfires

1. **Reporter:** Do you think it's going to rain?
Florida State University coach Bill Peterson: What do you think I am? A geologist?

> *conversation about whether or not bad weather would affect a big game*

2. And in Tennessee today, they had tennis-sized golf balls.

> *weather forecaster Cheryl Jones, KMBC-TV (Kansas City, Missouri)*

3. Doppler shows us no precipitation this morning over all of eastern North Carolina, so the wet dreams of yesterday are indeed dead.

> *weather forecaster, WCTI (Greenville, North Carolina)*

4. Today we'll have clouds and rain. The perfect combination for precipitation.

> *radio meteorologist giving his drive-time forecast*

5. Weather Today—Sun or Rain.
sign at a Calcutta, India, hotel desk

6. And it's warm and wet in the city this morning. Let's find out how Isabelle Lange is—warm and wet as well?
TV newsman, talking to the female weather forecaster

7. And for the rest of Europe this weekend, a lot of cloud around in the form of cloud.
weather forecaster Suzanne Charlton, BBC1

8. Fox 5 (New York) anchor Ernie Anastos: It takes a tough man to make a tender forecast.
Weather forecaster Nick Gregory: I guess that's me.
Anastos: Keep f∗∗∗ing that chicken!

9. Tomorrow: Gary and Cool
High Temp: 68
weather forecast shown on NY1 (New York City)

10. Little change in rain, and no chance of temperature.
weather forecaster Rick Jeffries, KTKT (Tucson)

THE TOP 10 STUPIDEST
Restaurant Names
That Just Don't Work
for Some Reason

1. The Golden Shower Restaurant
   Tanzania

2. Phat Phuc Noodle Bar
   England

3. Poon Palace
   Sweden

4. The Chocolate Log
   India

5. My Dung
   Vietnam

6. The Golden Stool
   England

7. Cum n Eat
   Northern Ireland

8. Poo de Poo
   Yamaguchi, Japan

9. Pumpkin Poo
   Japan

10. Spleen Café
   Italy

Not-Terribly-Helpful Helpful Hints

1. Never pour tea directly into your eyes.

advice column, Bangkok (Thailand) *Post*

2. [Call 911 and] say these words: "There has been a life-endangering emergency at the Department of Justice Exercise facility."

step one of a list of instructions posted in the Justice Department's Occupational Health and Physical Fitness Program Facility (i.e., gym)

3. Don't Make Luggage Look Like a Bomb

headline, El Paso (Texas) *Times*

4. *Printed inside a 6-inch plastic bag:* Do not climb inside this bag and zip it up. Doing so will cause injury or death.

5. Notice: Do not press any key when the following message appears: Press any key to boot from the CD.

Dell Dimension 2400 owner's manual

6. Don't go into darkened parking lots unless they are well-lighted.

crime specialist on television

7. In case of fire, evacuate the building.

Do not use stairways.

Do not use elevators.

sign by elevator in the Federal Reserve Bank Building, Boston

8. All you have to do [to protect yourself from nuclear radiation] is go down to the bottom of your swimming pool and hold your breath.

Department of Energy spokesperson David Miller

9. Follow the steps below to install AGP card: (Due to various design of AGP cards, please follow the installation guide that came with your AGP card and ignore the steps below)

on an Internet website

10. Please do not forget anything that you take with you.

automated announcement in Beijing taxi for customers leaving the cab

Bloviations about Things That Blow Up

1. I do not like this word "bomb." It is not a bomb. It is a device that is exploding.

> *French ambassador to New Zealand Jacques le Blanc, regarding press coverage of France's nuclear weapons tests in the Pacific*

2. Atomic Enema

> *name of product in Hong Kong, made by Benzene Chem and Pharm Ltd.*

3. And from the British battleships
a fierce cannonade did boom,
And continued from six in the morning
till two o'clock in the afternoon.
And by the 26th of July the guns of
Fort Moro were destroyed
And the French and Spaniards were
greatly annoyed.

> *from "The Capture of Havana" by William McGonagall (often termed the world's worst poet)*

4. When threats failed, he detonated his wife.

> *headline,* The Times of India

5. *Bombproof Your Horse*
   book title

6. Maurice Kearton can remember clearly falling near his home and failing to explode during the Second World War.
   Kent Today *(UK)*

7. Army Shifts Practice Bomb Runs at PTA
   headline, West Hawaii (Kailua-Kona) Today

8. *Explosive Spiders and How to Make Them*
   book title

9. I have Microsoft Exploder.
   caller to a tech help line

10. Butte Blast Blamed on Leaking Gas
   Associated Press headline

THE TOP 10 STUPIDEST
"Can't Argue with That" Statements

1. Osama Bin Laden would never understand the joys of Hanukkah.

> *President George W. Bush, in a speech at a menorah-lighting ceremony at the White House*

2. Wife's Family: Man Who Killed Family Not All Good

> *headline,* Anderson (South Carolina) Independent-Mail

3. I can promise you if we'd been 4-1 after those first five games, we wouldn't have ended up 3-8.

> *North Carolina football coach Carl Torbush, commenting on his team's bad 1-4 start*

4. Until you have him, you do not have him.

> *Secretary of Defense Donald Rumsfeld, on expectations that suspected Saudi terrorist Osama bin Laden would be captured soon*

5. We haven't had any more rain since it stopped raining.

> *tennis commentator Harry Carpenter*

6. Once he'd gone past the point of no return, there was no going back.

sportscaster, BBC1

7. The only way to get our economy going again and solve our budget problems is to get the economy moving.

Sen. John Boehner (R-Ohio)

8. One of the great unknown champions because very little is known about him.

sportscaster David Coleman

9. We lost because we didn't win.

soccer star Ronaldo

10. *Family Feud* **host Richard Dawson:** Name something that can kill a lively party.

Contestant: A gun.

Not-Very-Educated Quotes about Education

1. Rarely is the question asked, Is our children learning?

   President George W. Bush

2. Education tests who more effort needed in reading comprehension.

   Caledonian-Record *(St. Johnsbury, Vermont)*

3. Kiducation

   We turn old clothes into new kids

   through education

   ad for a nonprofit organization's clothing drive, Rhode Island

4. Excellance In Secondary Education

   banner in the Raleigh, North Carolina, room where an educational task force met to come up with ways to improve the state's SAT scores

5. New York City Department of Education preparatory guide: "Mathematics Planning for Forth Grade"

   title of New York City guidebook

6. Teacher Roger's Academy

   Awarded Internationally

   Graduated in singe 6 months

   ¡You do not waste you time with annoying rules!

   Learn as you learned the spanish and I gave in english everything what you mean

   Guaranteed

   ad for an English language school, Mazatlán, Mexico

7. More education is not a pancreas.

Mississippi state legislator, commenting on a proposed state education plan

8. Ten years ago, only a third of schoolchildren went on to higher education. Now it is 33 per cent.

teachers' spokesperson, UK

9. Burnham Category II/III courses may or may be advanced and poolable. A Burnham Category II/III course which is not poolable is not poolable only because it is not advanced, i.e. it does not require course approval as an advanced course. It is therefore wrong to ascribe it as a "non-poolable advanced (non-designated) course." Non-poolable courses are non-advanced by definition. I think that the problem you have described probably results from confusion here.

letter from the British Department of Education and Science, explaining courses

10. Math Book Used in Local Classroom

headline, Bellingham (Washington) Herald

THE TOP 10 STUPIDEST
Beauty Pageants

1. Miss Artificial Beauty

2. Miss Beauty in Epaulettes

3. Miss Captivity

4. Miss and Mister Beautiful Bottom

5. Miss Klingon Empire

6. Miss Turkey Trot and Drumsticks

7. Miss Mama Kilo

8. Miss Armpit Queen

9. Miss Mule Day

10. Miss Hooker

Gay-Related Articulations

1. I think that gay marriage should
be between a man and a woman.

> *California governor Arnold
> Schwarzenegger*

2. We're well aware of the male
homosexual problem in this
country, which is of course
minor, but to our certain
knowledge there is not one
lesbian in England.

> *Lord Chamberlain of England
> to Lillian Hellman, during
> a discussion of the play* The
> Children's Hour *(from* Lilly, *by
> Peter Feibleman)*

3. Reserves, National Guard: Who can keep them straight?

> *headline,* St. Louis (Missouri) Post-Dispatch

4. John Kennedy, chairman of Beaconsfield, said: "Mr Portillo's
statement about his homosexuality when he was at university
did not help at all. It put a lot of people off. The Conservative
Party doesn't really represent the average members of the country.
I am perfectly happy for people doing what they want behind closed
doors but I don't want them waving it about in public."

> *from a story in* The Times *(UK)*

5. Press Release

"The aggressive homosexual lobby appear to have their fingers into everything," stated a UK LifeLeague spokesman. . . .

from a UK LifeLeague Press Release

6. I believe that people like myself should stand shoulder to shoulder with the homosexual fraternity . . . but you're only likely to get that support if you don't continue to flaunt your homosexuality and thrust it down other people's throats.

British member of Parliament Geoffrey Dickens

7. Because the bishop of Harare would not condemn homosexuals, he is facing rearguard action.

broadcaster Peter Byles

8. Gay men have changed their sexual behavior, but it's extremely difficult to keep it up year after year.

British safe-sex group official Jamie Taylor

9. I don't mind gays. But I don't want them stuffing it down my throat all the time.

Utah state senator Chris Buttars (R-10th District), on a local Fox station

10. Now, Mark, this guy Tony that you share your life with—is he homosexual too?

*Philadelphia mayor Frank Rizzo, on his radio talk show
to a gay guest*

THE TOP 10 STUPIDEST,
Unpredictable, Strange, Otherworldly, and Otherwise Truly Alien Menu Items

1. Fried Convoluted Watch

   menu item, Hanoi, Vietnam

2. Chinstrap with get them

   menu item,
   Santiago, Spain

3. Anonymous Black Jelly

   menu item,
   Montien Hotel,
   Bangkok, Thailand

4. Stewed Language

   menu item,
   Madrid, Spain

5. Cocktails

   Strained fragmentation
   hand grenade: rum, cream of the
   Coco and fragmentation hand
   grenade drink

   menu item, Mojácar, Almeria, Spain

6. Fillet of Leather Jacket
in a saffron cream sauce and vegetables
menu item, Grappa's Country restaurant, Hong Kong

7. Fried Rice from Hell
menu item, Hanoi, Vietnam

8. gelatinous mutant coconut
menu item, South Korea

9. Indonesian Nazi Goreng
*menu item, At Village restaurant, Hong Kong, from its
"Exotic flavours of the Orient" menu section*

10. Torture Soup
menu item, Djerba, Tunisia

Questions Ever Asked

1. How did you guys run so slowly in that opening *Baywatch* scene . . . you know, where you were running down the beach?

  singer Jessica Simpson to Pamela Anderson

2. You definitely must feel like you didn't do anything wrong, I mean to write a book and whatever, like that's how secure you are that this is something else?

  journalist/blogger Meghan McCain, to former Illinois governor Rod Blagojevich when she was cohosting The View

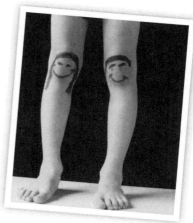

3. Is that a grimace of pain in his right knee?

  sportscaster David Coleman

4. My "Replace Battery" light is on, what should I do?

  from the "Frequently Asked Questions" list on American Power Conversion's website

5. When you said that, there was some hesitation. Have you heard of others that you haven't heard about yet?

  lawyer, in courtroom testimony

6. A red moon? Why don't you say "blue buttocks"?

   English subtitle in Hong Kong kung-fu movie

7. Did you tell the Subler doctor the same thing as you told the Smith Transfer doctor as you told the Subler doctor the first time when you had your second Subler physical?

   lawyer, in courtroom testimony

8. Was your home completely damaged, or was it destroyed?

   newscaster interviewing a displaced homeowner while covering a landslide in Laguna Beach, California

9. Two questions—why were England so poor? And if they were poor, why?

   sportscaster Ian Payne, covering the World Cup

10. **Tech support:** Type "fix," with an "f."
   Caller: Is that "f" as in "fix"?

THE TOP 10 STUPIDEST
Questions Ever Asked in Films

1. Cutting off her nipples with garden shears?
You call that normal?

> *Elizabeth Taylor, in* Reflections in a Golden Eye *(1967)*

2. How many times have I held your head over the toilet while
you threw up everything except your memories?

> *Cher to her star (drunk) dancer, in* Burlesque *(2010)*

3. We sold our bodies; why can't we sell
some wood?

> *Mary Stuart Masterson, in* Bad Girls
> *(1994)*

4. How could someone with such great
ideas for humanity put an innocent
woman in a pit?

> *Janet Julian as the heroine to Stephen
> Collins, in* Choke Canyon *(1986)*

5. How many of our neighbors have
their girlfriends' heads in their
freezers?

> *wife of philandering husband Peter
> Gallagher, in* Virtual Obsession
> *(1998)*

6. Isn't it strange how that lovely song reminds you of chicken salad?

aging spinster typist Joan Crawford to her young and looney lover Cliff Robertson about the title song, in Autumn Leaves *(1956)*

7. Have you ever been collared and dragged out in the street and thrashed by a naked woman?

Elizabeth Taylor as a frustrated wife, in Reflections in a Golden Eye *(1967)*

8. If I didn't really work for the government, if I was just a guy who accidentally killed his parents, would you still love me?

arsonist Anthony Perkins to schoolgirl Tuesday Weld, in Pretty Poison *(1968)*

9. Could you just promise if you eat me that you'll clean your plates?

worried plane crash survivor stranded in the snow-covered mountains, in Alive *(1993)*

10. And what are little boys made of? Is it snakes and snails and puppy dog tails? Or is it brassieres?! And corsets?!

narrator, in Glen or Glenda *(1953)*

Peculiarly Intriguing Headlines

1. Bush Urges Use of Condoms Based on Uganda Experience
   Taipei (Taiwan) Times

2. Thousands of False Eyelash Factory Workers Run Amok
   The Jakarta (Indonesia) Post

3. Two Mexican Midget Wrestlers Killed by Fake Prostitutes
   Fox News website

4. N. Korean Leader Names Ancient Frog "Ancient Frog"
   Bangkok (Thailand) Post

5. Ride a Giant Weiner to the Land of Smiles
   The Charlotte (North Carolina) News

6. Africa: Glamour. Decadence. Murder. Hundreds of Secretarial Opportunities
   Nine to Five *magazine*

7. Skydiver Lands on Beer Vendor at Women's Cole Slaw Wrestling Event
   Petersburg (Virginia) Progress-Index

8. Virgin Holds Off 10,000 in Peachtree
   Lewiston (Idaho) Morning Tribune, *about long-distance runner Craig Virgin's winning the Atlanta Peachtree Classic race*

9. Five-headed Coach to Lead Washington School
   The Wenatchee (Washington) World

10. Woman in Sumo Wrestler Suit Assaulted Her Ex-girfriend in Gay Pub after She Waved at Man Dressed as a Snickers Bar
   Evening Herald *(Dublin, Ireland)*

Time-Measurement Cognition Problems

1. Please excuse Andrea for being absent January 28th, 29th, 30th, 31st, 32nd and 33rd.

> *letter to a teacher in Thornton, Indiana, explaining a child's absence from school*

2. **Game show host Paul Wappat:** How long did the Six-Day War between Egypt and Israel last?

Contestant (after long pause): Fourteen days.

> *during a game show segment on BBC Radio Newcastle (UK)*

3. This week, the Saturday matinee will be held on Tuesday instead of Thursday.

> Wellsboro (Pennsylvania) Gazette

4. **Radio host Mike Parry:** How many Christmases took place during the Second World War?

Contestant: Fifty-eight.

5. Open 9 Days a Week

> *sign on store door*

6. *Are You Smarter Than a 10 Year Old?* **host Noel Edmonds:** How many days will there be in the year 2010?

Contestant: Er . . . is it 60 or 52?

7. Reporter: Will your injury keep you out for six weeks?
Baseball player Junior Ortiz: No, longer than that. Maybe a month and a half.

8. Filene's
One Day Sale!
This Friday, Saturday
and Sunday

*Filene's department
store ad, Connecticut*

9. There remain only twenty-five hours in the day, and Neil Kinnock is already working for twenty-three and a half of them.

British Labour Party spokesman Robin Cook

10. Male radio host: Guess how many hours sleep you lose in a year looking after a newborn baby.
Female host: What, in all 352 days?
Male host (laughing): Don't you mean 356?
Female host: Okay, in a leap year, right.

Real Radio (UK)

THE TOP 10 STUPIDEST

Philosophical Statements by Celebrities

1. I just think the more you can do to maximize your health while you're alive the better.

actress Gwyneth Paltrow

2. Take Ernest Hemingway: Here was a guy who swallowed, bit, and orally sucked on the long barrel of a shotgun. What does that tell you? What does it tell you when a guy—in one of the more exotic cases I have heard of—hugs a stove, a hot stove, to death? Horrifying. But what does that tell you?"

actor William Shatner

3. Elevator passenger: Where do you want to go?

Model Claudia Schiffer: I don't know. I've never been there.

conversation when Schiffer walked into the occupied elevator, hit a button that didn't light up because the floor was unoccupied, then continued to hold down the button

4. I guess I'm not really involving my imagination to that of a circumstance or happening—I'm just kind of acknowledging it as an existence.

actor Keanu Reeves, when reminded that the Art Center College of Design in Pasadena, California, was offering a Keanu Reeves film class

5. When I get lonely, I want to be alone. I like to indulge in my loneliness so I can figure out that I'm not really lonely.

actress Alicia Silverstone

6. We are all looking at how we have to shift, because you look at the good and you look at what's not working, and I think people, God bless it, are working in the consciousness, God bless it, that with all the problems out there in the world, how are we going to shift the consciousness?

designer Donna Karan

7. Changing someone's life is not the best, is not wanting to change the other life. It is being who you are that changes another's life. Do you understand?

actress Juliette Binoche

8. What would happen if you melted? You know, you never really hear this talked about that much, but spontaneous combustion? It exists! [People] burn from within. . . . Sometimes they'll be in a wooden chair and the chair won't burn, but there'll be nothing left of the person. Except sometimes the teeth. Or the heart. No one speaks about this—but it's for real.

actor Keanu Reeves

9. I feel my best when I'm happy.

actress Winona Ryder

10. You know, it really doesn't matter what [the media] write as long as you've got a young and beautiful piece of ass.

mogul Donald Trump

THE TOP 10
Stupidest-Sounding Lawsuits

1. Hamburger v. Fry

2. Fried v. Rice

3. Frankenstein v. Independent Roofing and Siding

4. Advance Whip & Novelty Co. v. Benevolent Protective Order of Elks

5. Friends of the Kangaroo Rat v. California Dept. of Corrections

6. U.S. v. Pipe on Head

7. Jones v. God, Jesus, Others

8. State v. Big Hair

9. Big v. Little

10. Short v. Long

THE TOP 10 STUPIDEST

Unfortunate Turns of Phrase

1. Butts Arrested in Boob Murder Case

headline, wearecentralpa.com (WTAJ-News website)

2. If you're going to get in behind Rio Ferdinand you've got to show him what you've got and then go in hard.

sports commentator Jamie Redknapp

3. Reverend John, who is living with an openly gay partner, is no doubt feeling rather sore today.

newscaster Paul Handley, Radio 5 Live (UK)

4. A man who keeps playing with himself in public has been told by a judge, "It is in your own hands, but you do need help."

newspaper story, Thanet Times *(UK)*

5. Royals to Get a Taste of Angel's Colon

headline, wsoctv.com (Charlotte, North Carolina)

6. We have seen that in this round that the Senators are having a hard time penetrating the end of Buffalo.

hockey announcer, The Team 1200 (Ottawa) covering a game

7. Governor's Penis Busy

headline in the New Haven (Connecticut) Register *(which should have read "Pen Is . . . ")*

8. They seem cold out there, they're rubbing each other and he's come in his shorts.

> *broadcaster Michael Buerk, watching colleague*
> *Philippa Forrester cuddle a male astronomer for warmth*
> *during BBC1's eclipse coverage*

9. Only Poets Can Save Us from Millennium Buggery

> *headline,* The Times of India, *referring to the so-called Y2K bug,*
> *which was supposed to cripple computers*

10. Seniors to Tour Morgue, Eat Ribs

> *headline,* Birmingham (Michigan) Eccentric

Things Said
By or About Evil Dictators
(Plus One Sidekick)

1. **Customer:** I'm looking for a copy of *Mein Kampf.*

   Bookseller: Is that the author?

   Customer: No, it's German for *My Struggle.* It's by Hitler.

   Bookseller: Hitler who?

   Customer: Are you serious?

   Bookseller (raising eyes in pained look): Look, I don't know *every* author in the world.

2. **Radio host Richard Bacon:** What artist had a blue period?

   Contestant: Stalin?

   on the Richard Bacon show, XFM

3. Yes, I would defend [Adolf Hitler]. And I would win.

   lawyer Alan Dershowitz

4. No one would go to Hitler's funeral if he was alive today.

    British member of Parliament Ron Brown

5. I know a lot of women who use men, but the world is not perfect. Fifty years ago there was Hitler; now there are bitches everywhere.

    actress Julie Delpy

6. *The Weakest Link* **host Anne Robinson:** In catering, a famous chain of tea shops and so-called "corner houses" was opened in London in 1894 by Joseph who?
Contestant: Goebbels.

7. *Family Fortunes* **host:** What is Hitler's first name?
Contestant: Heil.

8. Just to keep the record straight, it was the famous Whistler's Mother, not Hitler's that was exhibited in the recent meeting of the Pleasantville Methodists.

    The Titusville (Pennsylvania) Herald

9. Last Night I Dreamed of Chairman Mao

    Communist Chinese hit song

10. Why did we name it Hitler's Cross Restaurant? We wanted to be different. This is one name that will stay in people's minds.

    restaurant owner Punit Sablok, who later changed the name after a rather predictable public outcry

Idiotic Ideological Iterations

1. We have nothing against ideas. We're against people spreading them.

Chilean dictator General Augusto Pinochet

2. We are among the world leaders for semi-conductors, but with the power of communism, we will soon be able to be leaders for *full* conductors.

general secretary of the Czechoslovak communist party Milŏ Jakĕ

3. I can't believe that we are going to let a majority of the people decide what's best for this state!

Louisiana state representative John Travis, when opposing legislation that was popular with voters

4. We had to suspend elections to save democracy.

Algerian diplomat

5. I intend to open this country up to democracy, and anyone who is against that, I will jail, I will crush.

Brazilian president João Baptista de Oliveira Figueiredo

6. What right does Congress have to go around making laws, just because they deem it necessary?

Washington, D.C., mayor Marion Barry

7. **Reporter:** How soon do you expect Argentina to be returned to democratic government?

Argentine president Roberto Viola: We believe we are already within a democratic system. Some factors are still missing, like the expression of the people's will.

8. Where fraternities are not allowed, communism flourishes.

Sen. Barry Goldwater (R-Arizona), speaking before the National Interfraternity Conference

9. Democracy used to be a good thing, but now it has gotten into the wrong hands.

Sen. Jesse Helms (R-North Carolina)

10. Under the anti-social capitalist, the great mass of the people are victims of every kind of weather freak . . . the heat parches them and saps their energy and health. Only in the Soviet Union, where there is Socialism, are the rest, leisure and living conditions of the people fully provided for— these rights are written into the Stalin Constitution.

from the CPUSA-published paper Daily Worker, *1940*

THE TOP 10 STUPIDEST
Actual Book Titles

1. *A Toddler's Guide to the Rubber Industry*

2. *Constipation and Our Civilization*

3. *Greek Rural Postmen and Their Cancellation Numbers*

4. *The Secret of Sphincters*

5. *A Pictorial Book of Tongue Coating*

6. *Life and Laughter 'midst the Cannibals*

7. *Be Bold with Bananas*

8. *Hand-Grenade Throwing as a College Sport*

9. *Collect Fungi on Stamps*

10. *A Study of Hospital Waiting Lists in Cardiff, 1953–1954*

So Hip It Hurts
Film Lines

1. Christy, what is this jazz you puttin' down about our planet being round? Everybody hip that it's square!

> *cool teen, paraphrasing what Queen Isabella said to Columbus, in* High School Confidential! *(1958)*

2. Real crazy. These footprints go in a circle. Maybe the natives here are getting on this rock 'n' roll kick.

> *hip guy when he and his buddies discover sinister footprints on the desert island they're stranded on, in* She Demons *(1958)*

3. **Girl:** Don't look at me like that. I can read your head. Dolly and Patty have nothing to do with thee and me.

Guy: I don't . . . I don't wanna hear any more about them dykes. And if you don't cool this lickety-split-talk-talk jazz, you're gonna get my paranoid goin' too, ya dig?

> *beatnik girl and her boyfriend, discussing two lesbians at another table, in* Once a Thief *(1965)*

4. You know what I want to be? Nothing, you dig? If you can't dig "nothing," you can't dig anything. Dig?

> *Stash the hippie, in* Skidoo *(1968)*

5. I'm dying to blast but I'm clean. Are you holding?

> *cute co-ed who's looking for some marijuana, in* High School Confidential! *(1958)*

6. Why is the good ass never radical and the radical ass never good?

Hippie student complaining in with-it '60s movie, R.P.M. *(1970)*

7. **The Prince:** If you leave, ya know what you are? You're the prunes.

Buzz Cameo: Prunes? You're the dunes.

The Prince: Yeah. You're the real prunes.

Brooklyn thug leader The Prince (Norman Mailer) and a cohort, in Mailer's Wild 90 *(1967)*

8. You can't expect me to let you go trippin' in a messed-up plane, do ya?

acid guide, in The Trip *(1967)*

9. If you flake around with the weed, you'll wind up doing the hard stuff.

High School Confidential! *(1958)*

10. Heck, yeah! I mean "hell, yeah." I say "hell" all the time!

Kayla, in the American Idol *film* From Justin to Kelly *(2003)*

Inadvertent References
to
Solid Bodily Functions

1. Moorpark Residents Enjoy a Communal Dump

California newspaper headline

2. Jeff Bagwell appears to have this invisible stool underneath his rear end.

sportscaster Tim McCarver referring to Jeff Bagwell's squatlike batting stance during the 1999 All-Star Game

3. He has popped out to the toilet to compose himself before the final push.

*sportscaster
Steve Davis*

4. Was that one of the more satisfying dumps you've had?

*sideline reporter
Suzy Shuster to
Nebraska head
coach Bill Callahan,
after he was doused
with Gatorade*

5. The farmers in Annapolis Valley are pleased to announce that this year there will be an abundance of apples. This is particularly good news because most of the farmers haven't had a good crap in years.

Maryland television news broadcaster during an early morning report

6. Spending on federal benefit programs is growing at an excremental rate.

Rep. Frank Guarini (D-New Jersey)

7. Many farmers are engaged in maple tree cultivation in the environs of Montreal and have whole groves of them. The species concerned is the sugar maple whose sap is particularly tasty and rich in sugar. . . . The syrup must be boiled, defecated, and evaporated as a result of which it becomes thick and sweet.

Czechoslovak Airlines in-flight magazine OK Flight

8. Well, I see in the game in Minnesota that Terry Felton has relieved himself on the mound in the second inning.

sportscaster Fred White, reading a wire-service summary that mistakenly showed the same starter and relief pitcher for the Minnesota Twins

9. House keeping: Cleaning, defecating, sterilizing for new residence
Floor maintaining face-lifting polishing to kitchen and toilet
Carpet cleaning: Clean, defecate, maintain all kinds of carpet

ad for the Mei Ao Labour Service cleaning service, in Beijing Today

10. • Large brown stool ambulating in the hall.

• Stool remains quite spry and active.

as recorded on hospital medical charts, as reported by Nursing *magazine*

THE TOP 10 STUPIDEST

Warning Labels
We Never Knew We Needed

1. *Warning label in electric thermometer instructions:*
   Do not use orally after using rectally.

2. *Warning label on fishing lure:*
   Dardevle Fishing Lure: Harmful if Swallowed

3. *Warning label on furniture cleaning cloths:*
   Furniture Wipes: Do Not Use
   as Baby Wipes

4. *Warning label on small tractor:*
   Danger: Avoid Death

5. *Warning label on a mattress:*
   Do not attempt to swallow

6. *Warning label on letter opener:*
Caution: Safety goggles recommended.

7. *Warning label on Vanishing Fabric Marker marking pen:*
The Vanishing Fabric Marker should not be used as
a writing instrument for signing checks or any
legal documents.

8. *Warning label on a CD player box:*
Warning—dangerous warning inside

9. *Warning label on "Popcorn Rock" decorative rock garden set:*
Eating rocks may lead to broken teeth.

10. *Warning label on a Taiwanese blanket:*
This blanket is not to be used as protection from
a tornado.

And Spaciest Things Ever Said about Outer Space

1. [It's] time for the human race to enter the solar system.

> *Vice President Dan Quayle, on the concept of a manned mission to Mars*

2. ***The Weakest Link* host Anne Robinson:** What force of nature is responsible for keeping the Earth, planets, and asteroids in orbit around the sun?

Contestant: Delta Force.

3. I'll have my first Zambian astronaut on the Moon by 1965, using my own firing system, derived from the catapult. . . . I'm getting them acclimatized to space travel by placing them in my space capsule every day. It's a 40-gallon oil drum in which they sit, and then I roll them down a hill. This gives them the feeling of rushing through space. I also make them swing from the end of a long rope. When they reach the highest point, I cut the rope—this produces free fall.

> *Edward Makuka Nkoloso, director general of the Zambia National Academy of Space Research in 1964*

4. 99 Congratulations Neil Armstrong on winning your 9th Tour de France.

> Las Vegas Sun *ad from the 99¢ shop*

5. Scientists spot plant outside Solar System

> *headline,* The Daily Chronicle *(Dekalb, Illinois)*

6. Game show host: Which mathematician said "The most incomprehensible thing about this universe is that it's comprehensible"?

Contestant: Mel Gibson.

from the 2BL 702 show, Australia

7. For NASA, space is still a high priority.

Vice President Dan Quayle

8. My vision is to make the most diverse state on Earth, and we have people from every planet on the Earth in this state, ah, we have the sons and daughters of people from every planet, of every country on Earth, in this state.

*California governor
Gray Davis*

9. Astronaut Takes Blame for Gas in Spacecraft

newspaper headline

10. "One small step for man, one giant leap for mankind. . . ." Powerful first words from Louis Armstrong, U.S. Astronaut and first man on the moon.

from an article in Siliconindia *magazine*

THE TOP 10 STUPIDEST

Quotes from an Alternate Reality (in Which Time and Space Appear to Have No Meaning)

1. Because of our taping schedule, this show will take place three weeks after you see it.

sportscaster Don Gillis

2. Something that I was not aware that happened suddenly turned out not to have happened.

British prime minister John Major

3. Nothing means nothing, but it isn't really nothing because nothing is something that isn't.

basketball player Darryl Dawkins

4. Continued from tomorrow

subheadline on a newspaper story, The Island *(Sri Lanka)*

5. That's twice that has happened in the recent future.
racing commentator Murray Walker

6. He has to start a little bit better than he has already begun.
sportscaster David Pleat

7. Payment Before Ordering
sign at restaurant in Ben Gurion Airport, Israel

8. I'm currently writing a screenplay that I haven't started yet.
tennis player Serena Williams

9. We're a long way from being where we are.
soccer player Steven Gerrard

10. I would still invade Iraq even if Iraq never existed.
President George W. Bush

ANOTHER TOP 10 STUPIDEST

Similes, Muddled Metaphors, and Confused Clichés

1. I can see the carrot at the end of the tunnel.
   sportscaster Stuart Pearce

2. He'll give you the bird's-eye view straight from the horse's mouth.
   radio host John McCauley

3. You can lead a horse to water, but you can't stick his head in it.
   baseball player Paul Owens

4. A zebra cannot change its spots.
   Vice President Al Gore, attacking President George H. W. Bush

5. No man is an Ireland.
   Chicago mayor Richard Daley

6. That's just the tip of the ice-cube.
   British member of Parliament Neil Hamilton

7. It appears as though the Achilles' heel of the Eagles' defense is about to rear its ugly head.
   sportscaster, covering a Philadelphia Eagles–Miami Dolphins game

8. It's a double-headed sword.
   basketball player Gilbert Arenas

9. We have to belly up to the buzz saw, and I think we're reaping the whirlwind from it.
   Sen. Jim Sasser (D-Tennessee)

10. We've got to ride this horse until the wheels come off.
   football player Steve Smith, on his team's third overtime win

Inappropriately Risqué Classified Ads

1. Ideally you will be of graduate caliber with at least two years' experience in Pubic Relations.

>*help wanted ad,*
>*the Telegraph Group*

2. Spacious 1554 sq. ft. home with large lot, family room with fireplace, huge dick for entertaining & enjoying the views. . . .

>*real estate ad, Redding,*
>*California, flyer*

3. Horse Share. Kind sensible adult—required to ride well behaved school mistress.

>*classified ad,* Beckenham (UK)
>News Shopper

4. Rear End. Slight crack, $50. Good condition.

>Pennysaver *ad listing (it*
>*should have read "Mustang*
>*Rear End")*

5. Large Dark brown wooden wardrobe and matching toy boy.

>*classified ad,* Penwith Pirate *(UK)*

6. Academic Kent male, N/S, Christian, selling house seeks tall sphincter, with no family ties, mature or older.

personal ad, Adscene, *Kent, England*

7. Notice: Will care for your dog while you are on vacation or during mating.

job wanted ad, Enigma, Georgia

8. A Private World—For you & your dong. See this cozy 1-2 bedroom home with its own fenced-dog run. Owner wants it Sold Now!

real estate ad, Pennsylvania newspaper

9. Rent 2 bedroom cottage high on mountain in St. John overlooking British Virgins.

real estate ad, Los Angeles, newspaper

10. Modular sofas. Only $299. For rest or fore play.

classified ad, Chicago newspaper

Frighteningly Moronic Game Show Moments

1. *Breakfast Show* **host Alan Brazil:** What was the name of the first man on earth?

Contestant: Tony.

on TalkSPORT (UK)

2. *The Big Quiz* **host Gary King:** What is the main ingredient of a Molotov cocktail?

Contestant: Vodka?

The Big Quiz, LBC

3. *Are You Smarter Than a 10 Year Old?* **host:** Along with two fishes, how many loaves of bread did Jesus use to feed the five thousand?

Contestant: When this question first came up, I thought four, but now I think it may have been six. It could have been eight, but now 14 seems to ring a bell.

4. *The Weakest Link* **host Anne Robinson:** What surname was shared by a historical outlaw called "Butch" and a fictional cowboy called "Hopalong"?

Contestant: Lesbian.

5. **BBC Radio Leeds host Graham Liver:** What piece of essential household equipment was invented by Thomas Crapper?

Contestant: Er . . .

Liver: The clue's in the question. Thomas Crapper.

Contestant: The tin opener?

6. **Radio host Johnny Hero:** What "R" is Hillary Clinton's middle name?

Contestant: Er, um, is it Rottweiler?

Downtown Radio, Northern Ireland

7. ***Family Feud* host Richard Dawson:** Name something you might accidentally leave on all night.

Contestant: Your shoe.

8. **Game show host Terry Wogan:** Which season is said to start on solstice day in December?

Contestant 1: Spring?

Wogan: In *December*, for God's sake!

Contestant 2: Summer?

Wogan's Perfect Recall

9. ***The Weakest Link* host Anne Robinson:** What William discovered that blood circulates around the body?

Contestant: Shatner.

10. ***Family Feud* host Richard Dawson:** Name an invention that has replaced stairs.

Contestant: The wheel.

THE TOP 10 STUPIDEST
Things Said About or to God

1. God, you are a finalist for the $11 million top prize. God, we've been searching for you. What an incredible fortune there would be for God! Could you imagine the looks you'd get from your neighbors? But don't just sit there, God.

> *part of a letter to God from the American Family Publishers, sent to God at the Bushnell Assembly of God in Bushnell, Florida, saying that God was a finalist for the $11 million top prize*

2. Marxism
God's Favored Coffee!

> *ad for instant coffee, Korea*

3. God Gets a Parking Caution: "No Exceptions" Say Police

> *headline,* York & Wetherby District Advertiser *(UK)*

4. I can't perceive God being on the mound in the ninth inning and saying [a loss] is the way it should be. I perceive Him as being an individual who would beat you any way he can as long as it's within the rules.

> *baseball manager Dick Balderson*

5. *Dialogue in American film:*
That's when I got my call from God.
Subtitle as it appeared in Europe:
That's when God telephoned me.

6. Lonely God potato twists
   snack food, China

7. He don't have no problem with you blinging. God's heavenly abode proves that he is the real king of bling. His gates are pearly, his house is about 10 stadiums big, the streets are gold. You do the budget on that kind of place.
   rapper Mase

8. *Cooking with God*
   cookbook title

9. God was the first Kiwanian.
   Rev. W. F. Powell, speaking before the Kiwanis Club of Columbus

10. Statue of God the Father. Approximately life-size.
   from a catalog of antiques for sale, as printed in the Evening Standard *(London)*

THE TOP 10 STUPIDEST
Distinctly Dumb Distinctions

1. There is no prostitution in China, however, we do have some women who make love for money.

> *Chinese Foreign Ministry spokesperson*

2. I haven't committed a crime. What I did was fail to comply with the law.

> *New York City mayor David Dinkins, answering accusations that he failed to pay his taxes*

3. There was not a breach of security as such. It was a case of someone cutting a hole from the outside and facilitating the escape of three of our inmates.

> *governor of a prison in Derek, England*

4. Don't say I don't get along with my teammates. I just don't get along with some of the guys on the team.

> *football player Terrell Owens*

5. Staff members do not have chauffeurs. . . . They have aides who drive.

> *New Jersey governor's chief of staff Lewis Thurston*

6. It's not censorship. It's just removing it from a library.

Eddie MacCausland, Marion County, Florida, library advisory board member, defending his proposal to ban a sex education book from the public library

7. It's not the amendment with which I disagree. It's the contents of the amendment.

Louisiana state representative Naomi Farve (D-New Orleans)

8. It's not true [the Congressman was sleeping during the debate]. He was just taking a few moments for deep reflection.

aide to Rep. Martin Hoke (R-Ohio), seen on the House floor with eyes closed during the debate on Contract with America

9. PETA isn't saying don't wear fur. They're saying don't abuse animals and so I'm not abusing animals. I'm just wearing a fur.

The Real Housewives of New York City star Kelly Bensimon

10. I don't own an SUV. The family has it. I don't have it.

Sen. John Kerry (D-Massachusetts), when asked on Earth Day if he owned a gas-guzzling SUV

Problems with Single-Digit Counting

1. Eddie Robinson is about one word: winning and losing.

agent Paul Collier, after Robinson's release from the Chicago Bulls

2. Remember, there's only one taxpayer—you and me.

Calgary city councilman John Kushner

3. I'll tell you, it's Big Business. If there is one word to describe Atlantic City, it's Big Business.

business magnate Donald Trump

4. Broadcaster John Humphries: So, in one word, don't get rid of the lottery, do it better?

Broadcaster Sue Lawley: That was two words.

5. I've only got two words: It ain't no surprise.

football player Darrien Gordon

6. The single most important two things we can do . . .

British prime minister Tony Blair

7. I hope that history will present me with maybe two words. One is peace. The other is human rights.

President Jimmy Carter

8. There are two ways of getting the ball—one way is from your own players, and that's the only way.

soccer manager Terry Venables

9. Judge: What inspired you to make this invention?
Contestant: Two words: nachos.

on a reality show for would-be inventors

10. Lleyton Hewitt . . . his two greatest strengths are his legs, his speed, his agility, and his competitiveness.

tennis commentator Pat Cash

THE TOP 10 STUPIDEST
Bee Comments

1. I never would have dreamed it would turn out to be the bees! They've always been our friends!

> *entomologist Brad Crane, warning the world of peril, in* The Swarm *(1978)*

2. **DJ**: What creature squirts a smelly unpleasant fluid at its enemies?

Contestant: A snake.

DJ: No, I'll give you a clue—it's black and white.

Contestant: A bee.

> *game show on Capital Radio (UK)*

3. **Army officer:** You're doing *what*? Are you mad? You mean you want us to conduct peace negotiations with BUGS? With BEES?

Scientist: Either that, or you can consider praying!

> The Bees *(1978)*

4. The African killer bee portrayed in this film bears absolutely no relationship to the industrious, hard-working American honey bee to which we are indebted for pollinating vital crops that feed our nation.

> *title card at the end of* The Swarm *(1978)*

5. All bees entering Kentucky shall be accompanied by certificates of health.

> *Kentucky statute 252.130 Law39*

6. With its highly evolved social structure of tens of thousands of worker bees commanded by Queen Elizabeth, the honey bee genome could also improve the search for genes linked to social behavior. . . . Queen Elizabeth has ten times the life span of worker bees and lays up to 2,000 eggs a day.

> *Reuters online news article*

7. The peasant is like a wild flower in the forest, and the revolutionary like a bee. Neither can survive or propagate without the other. There is one essential difference between us and the bees, however. In this hive, I *will not* tolerate drones!

> *Che Guevara to his rag-tag rebel army, in* Che! *(1969)*

8. *Anorexia Nervosa in Bulgarian Bees*

> *book title, as collected by* Bookseller *magazine for its annual Oddest Title of the Year award*

9. High Cholesterol Linked to Excessive Bee Diet, Top Dietitian Asserts

> *newspaper headline*

10. No! Not the bees! Nooooo! Not the bees! My eyes! Arghhhhhhh! Arghhhhhh! Arghhhhhh!

> *Edward Malus, in* The Wicker Man *(2006)*

THE TOP 10 STUPIDEST
Typically Bureaucratic Definitions

1. *Exit access:* that part of a means of egress that leads to an entrance to an exit
    U.S government fire-prevention pamphlet distributed at nursing homes

2. *Hammer:* manually powered fastener driving impact device
    U.S. Department of Defense

3. *Tent:* frame-supported tension structure
    U.S. Department of Defense

4. *Road signs:* ground-mounted confirmatory route markers
    Massachusetts Department of Public Works

5. *Factory shutdown:* volume-related production schedule adjustment
    General Motors

6. *Fire someone:* implement a lean concept of synchronous organizational structures
    Corporate human resources

7. *Emergency shelter for families:* an emergency shelter which shelters families
    Columbus (Ohio) Coalition for the Homeless

8. *Homelessness:* the state or condition of being a homeless person
    Columbus (Ohio) Coalition for the Homeless

9. *Clear cut forests:* temporary meadows
    U.S. Forest Service

10. *Toothpick:* wood interdental stimulator
    U.S. Department of Defense

THE TOP 10 STUPIDEST
(and Least Romantic) Romantic Remarks

1. When I'm sitting here with you, I don't even think about slime people . . .

hero to heroine, in The Slime People *(1963)*

2. FROM: Oregon Knife Shop
SENT: Tuesday, February 06, 2007 10:25 AM
TO:
SUBJECT: Say I love you with a knife . . . and free shipping. Valentines Day Knife Sale.

e-mail

3. ***Family Feud* host Richard Dawson:** . . . a romantic sounding musical instrument?

Contestant: Drum.

4. I paid off a poker debt with sexual favors and fell in love. It's so romantic.

actress Pamela Anderson, on her now ex-husband, Rick Salomon

5. If you had no idea what to get her for Valentine's Day . . . Give her the perfect gift, make pre-arrangements as a couple with the affordable funeral home.

funeral home ad

6. **Reporter:** When did you get married?

Basketball player Tyrone Hill (turning to his publicist): When did I get married?

7. *The Romance of Leprosy*
The Romance of Proctology
Truncheons: Their Romance and Reality
    book titles

8. Reporter: What's it like pitching in late innings?
Pitcher Daniel Bard: The only thing that compares to it is shooting a big deer, or maybe getting married.

9. "I love you only" Valentine's Day cards: Now available in multi-packs!
    sign on a card shop display

10. Elias Sime, one of the most prolific artists of our time, asks the timeless question "What is Love?" by using goats as a metaphor to explore perceptions and ideas of love.
    in a Cultural Program brochure of the Alliance Ethio-Française, Addis Ababa, Ethiopia

THE TOP 10 STUPIDEST
"I Didn't Know *That*" Newspaper Headlines

1. Cloudy Weather in Phoenix Caused by Clouds Says Grant
   Phoenix (Arizona) Republican

2. Cold Weather Causes Temperature to Drop
   The Stillwater (Oklahoma) News-Press

3. Reason for More Bear Sightings: More Bears
   Akron newspaper

4. In College Ball, Parity Is the Great Equalizer
   The Washington Post

5. Silent plane would cut airport noise
   cnn.com

6. Drowning Can Ruin Fun in Water, Council Warns
   Marshalltown (Iowa) Times-Republican

7. "Light" meals are lower in fat, calories
   The Herald-Dispatch *(Huntington, Alabama)*

8. Biting nails can be sign of tenseness in a person
   The Daily Gazette *(Schenectady, New York)*

9. How We Feel About Ourselves Is the Core of Self-Esteem Says Author Louise Hart
   Daily Camera *(Boulder, Colorado)*

10. Bible Church's Focus Is the Bible
   St. Augustine (Florida) Record

Excessively Politically Correct Statements

1. An item in Thursday's Nation Digest about the Massachusetts budget crisis made reference to new taxes that will help put Massachusetts "back in the African American." The item should have said "back in the black."
> *correction notice, in the* Fresno (California) Bee

2. Hello. This is Women in Entertainment. Our office will be personned again on Monday, the 24th of October.
> *answering machine at Women in Entertainment*

3. The snowman is, of course, white and invariably male. [His] ritual location in the semi-public space of garden or field imaginatively reinforces a spatial social system, marking women's proper sphere as the domestic-private and men's as the commercial-public. . . . It presents an image, however jocular, of a masculine control of public space.
> *University of Birmingham (UK) art historian Tricia Cusack*

4. These are times that try men's souls and women's souls.
> *Sen. Don Riegle (D-Michigan)*

5. Atomic Bombers Upset Over Enola Homosexual Exhibit
> *headline in the* Northwest Herald *(Crystal Lake, Illinois), referring to the Smithsonian Institution's planned exhibit on the dropping of the atomic bomb on Hiroshima by the plane the Enola Gay*

6. I consider myself the Susan B. Anthony of wrestling.
> *WWF wrestler Chyna*

7. What we are about is moving from androcentric values and behaviors to androgynous or better yet (for consciousness raising) gyandrous health care and societal values. In the process, the health occupations must be desexigrated. . . .

> *NOW president in a letter to the director of the Center for Women in Medicine*

8. I couldn't get over the fact that there was no difference between [famous soul food restaurant] Sylvia's restaurant and any other restaurant in New York City. I mean, it was exactly the same, even though it's run by blacks, primarily black patronship. . . . There wasn't one person in Sylvia's who was screaming, "M-Fer, I want more iced tea."

> *TV show host Bill O'Reilly, after dining with Rev. Al Sharpton at the famous Harlem restaurant*

9. Flag-flying is a blatantly sexist phallic ritual. The symbolism of raising and lowering the flag once a day is obvious.

> *Women's Action Group, New Zealand*

And 1 That's Trying but Isn't Quite Making It

10. I don't think having a naked woman strapped to a rack is sexist at all. And I don't think the fact that we pretend to slit her throat is violent.

> *rocker Blackie Lawless*

Candies

1. **Coming Lemon**
   lemon squares candy, Japan

2. **Creamy Ball**
   chocolate bar, Japan

3. **Cloetta Plopp**
   chocolate caramel bar, Czech Republic

4. **Mental**
   mints, France

5. **Swine**
   China

6. **Chocolate Collon**
   chocolate-filled wafer, Japan

7. **Snot from the Nose of the Great Buddha**
   puffed rice candy, Japan

8. **Crap's Chocolate**
   chocolate bar, France

9. **Asse**
   chocolate nougat bits, Japan

10. **Spunk**
    salt licorice, Denmark

Sportscaster On-Air Moments

1. Here's Hodge on the breakaway! He's all by himself . . . he shoots . . . and Hodge missed the goal! He'll be thinking about that one for a while! Just look at the expression on Hodge's stick!

> *WSBK-TV sportscaster, on-air during a Boston Bruins hockey game*

2. Next up is Fernando Gonzalez, who isn't playing tonight.

> *sportscaster Jerry Coleman*

3. And now stand by for a running of the exciting annual race car event, the Grand Pricks . . . er, the Grand Pee . . . however you pronounce it. I'll give you the spelling and you take your choice. Grand P-R-I-X.

> *sportscaster*

4. The left foot sees it and hits it out of the air!

> *sportscaster Ron Atkinson*

5. That youngster is playing well beyond his 19 years . . . that's because he's 21.

> *sportscaster David Begg*

6. Matt Taylor is off—and what a chance he had. Two chances—three in fact, actually, if you count the third.

sportscaster Gary Weaver, covering a soccer game

7. . . . and Edson Arantes do Nascimento, commonly known as Pelé, hands his award to Damon Hill, commonly known as, uh, uh, Damon Hill.

sportscaster Murray Walker

8. Both quarterbacks are not showing their balls, uh . . . shy of throwing the balls, uh, ball.

sportscaster Pat Summerall, during a Minnesota-Dallas game of the NFL Championship playoffs

9. Today Pittsburgh beat the Pirates, 6 to 6!

sportscaster Vince Sculley, on-air during a Dodgers-Astros game, announcing results of a Pittsburgh Pirates–Chicago Cubs game

10. **Sportscaster Al Michaels:** Well, it appears that he has pulled his groin.

Sportscaster John Madden: And it's a shame, it's such a great groin.

during a Monday Night Denver Broncos game

THE TOP 10 STUPIDEST

Things You Never Wanted to Know about Celebrities but They Feel Compelled to Tell You

1. I'm holding so much water now I have a backside that looks like a cauliflower. And other parts of my body resemble strange vegetables like squashes or things like that.

> *actress Kate Winslet*

2. I didn't feel well earlier. That's why I fit into this dress. I was actually in the toilet all day.

> *actress Jennifer Lopez, who was wearing a very tight dress at a premiere party*

3. Whenever I get a little poo on my hands, I take a quick whiff of it, just in case it might be chocolate.

> *twitter written by singer Jason Mraz*

4. I once had really bad diarrhea at a Playboy autograph signing. I was squeezed into a tight red dress, dripping in sweat, and knew something was not right. But blonde model's heroic attempts to ignore it were sadly in vain. I just kept having my picture taken with the fans. But then I was like: "Oh no, the demon is about to be unleashed." And it was unleashed for about 20 guys to witness.

> *actress Jenny McCarthy*

5. I'm proud I still have a really good sex life with David. He is very much in proportion. He does have a huge one, though. He does. You can see it in the advert. It is all his. It is like a tractor exhaust pipe!

> *singer/designer Victoria Beckham*

6. I took a poo in the woods hunched over like an animal. It was awesome.

> *actress Drew Barrymore, after traveling to an impoverished village for an MTV environmental special*

7. Making love in the morning got me through morning sickness— I found I could be happy and throw up at the same time.

> *actress Pamela Anderson*

8. When we measured heads in eighth grade, mine was the biggest.

> *actress Marilu Henner*

9. When I got through with the twin pregnancy, my abdominal skin was such that I had to fold it up and then stick it in my pants.

> *actress Cybill Shepherd*

10. My self-administered enema demystified me; that's why I did it. There was something very liberating about it.

> *singer Kim Wilde*

THE TOP 10 STUPIDEST
Letters

1. Please feel free to contact me with other matters that are of importance to you. I am honored to serve as your representative in the U.S. Congress. i think you're an asshole.

Sincerely, Jo Ann Emerson
   Member of Congress

P.S. Please forgive the delay in responding.

> *letter sent to constituent by Rep. Jo Ann Emerson (R-Missouri), who said she had no idea how the last line got added and immediately launched an investigation*

2. Dear Customers, We earnestly hope that you will not enjoy every one moment of your visit in our Marketing Plaza.

> *direct mail letter sent to visitors who tour Sanyo, the Japanese electronics firm*

3. Thank you for telling us about your experience with Gillette cartridges. . . . I would like to arrange to send you none with our compliments.

> *reply from the Gillette Company to a complaint letter*

4. Dear Mr. Cook:

We have attempted on several occasions to reach you by telephone to discuss payment of your telephone account—which was recently disconnected.

> *letter sent from the phone company*

5. Important Notice To All Tenants

I am writing to advise tenants to take care when they are putting their heads out the window for any reason. There is a danger that you may get struck by some falling missionary.

letter sent by the Manchester council to tenants of apartment building

6. Lastly we are, for your kind consideration, as above ordered, we are really hopping this will be the first step of a long and successful copulation.

PR letter from Kanungsuk car rental service in Bangkok

7. Dear Education Program Member:

The pace thickens!

letter from the Education Program of Barnard College

8. If there is anything we can do to assist and help you, please do not contact us.

letter given to guests at the Howard Plaza Hotel, Taipei

9. Dear Sir:

We're writing to share some exciting news. As of July 9, 2007, you have 0 miles in your SkyMiles account.

direct mail letter from Delta SkyMiles

10. It is our firm belief that your visit and stay here will be worthwhile and forgettable.

letter from the mayor of Dalian, China, inviting potential guests to his city

THE TOP 10 STUPIDEST
Film Dialogue
Understatements

1. What a crazy day! The first time I've seen you in three years and we're buried alive!

> *woman making conversation with an old boyfriend, in* Cave-In *(1979)*

2. Boy: She got lost in the pyramids. The mummy will have her for supper!

Girl: Oh, the poor kid!

> *boy reporting his girlfriend is lost in the Mexican hinterlands,*
> *in* Wrestling Women vs. the Aztec Mummy *(1964)*

3. Businesswoman (after her lunch partner was savaged by mutant slugs): God! You never saw anything like what happened in that restaurant.

Businessman: Oh, put it out of your mind, Sue!

Businesswoman: How? His whole face was . . .

Mayor: Uh, can I freshen your drinks?

Businesswoman: I sure hope things like that don't happen around here again!

> Slugs: The Movie *(1988)*

4. Daughter: I was in an orgy. I was a stripper. I was a streetwalker. Then in a motel a man tried to forcibly seduce me.

Mother: There, there, dear. If you think these things are bad, wait till your children grow up.

> The Swinger *(1966)*

5. Hospital orderly: She was suffering from paranoia and hallucinations, induced by tranquilizers, cocaine, amphetamines, alcohol . . .

Mother (shrugging): She's always been difficult.

> The Lonely Lady *(1983)*

6. Man: I'd like to take you out in a monster-free city.

Woman: I'd like that.

> *discussion between man and woman as they look out the skyscraper window at a giant flying monster on a nest, in* Gamera: Guardian of the Universe *(1995)*

7. It's great to eat under an open sky, even if it is radioactive.

> *Frankie Avalon, enjoying a picnic with the family in after-the-nuclear-holocaust Los Angeles, in* Panic in the Year Zero! *(1962)*

8. Roxy: Dad, I can't describe it, but I know something has happened to him. He's a creature—why, you just have to look at him to see that! But I know, whatever he is, he's a human being.

Mr. Miller: You just can't get him out of your mind, huh?

> *father and daughter, discussing the monster man who had kidnapped her, in* Eegah *(1962)*

9. Murderers! They're all alike. Society would be better off without them!

> *prison guard, expressing his own opinion, in* Diary of a Madman *(1963)*

10. Girl: Excuse me—how far is it to Camp Crystal Lake?

Waitress: What is it, Enis, about twenty miles?

Truck driver: About that.

Local woman: Camp *Blood*? They're opening that place again?

> Friday the 13th *(1980)*

Not-Very-Eloquent Moments in Political Speeches

1. The argument about the Labor destroying any prospects of recovery may be déjà vu here . . . It's certainly not déjà vu in the country. It's very much vu. It's very much what, er . . . It's very much, er . . . shows what sort of education I've had.

British member of Parliament Chris Patten

2. People don't want hand outs! People want hand jobs!

Connecticut governor William O'Neill at a political rally, followed by riotous applause

3. Anxietyship is no substitute for leadership.

Rep. Jim Leach (R-Iowa)

4. It's time to put our blood or our urine where our mouth is.

Iowa state representative and Speaker of the Iowa house Pat Murphy, referring to drug testing

5. It is as throughout all Alaska that big wild good life teeming along the road that is north to the future.

Alaska governor Sarah Palin, in her resignation speech

6. My friends, no matter how rough the road may be, we can and we will never, never surrender to what is right.

Vice President Dan Quayle

7. . . . and there are the two major promises he has not been able to keep. And those are the promises to put more Americans back to work and the second promise is to, uh [pause] what is that second promise?

Secretary of State James Baker

8. And so, in my State of the—my State of the Union—or state—my speech to the nation, whatever you want to call it, speech to the nation—I asked Americans to give 4,000 years—4,000 hours over the next—the rest of your life—of service to America.

President George W. Bush

9. People say the war in Iraq is comparable to the Spanish Civil War, and the war in Iraq, to the larger war against Islamist terrorism, comparable to the Spanish Civil War, to the Second World War, the late '30s and the failure to grasp the growing threat of fascism in Europe until it was almost too late.

Sen. Joe Lieberman (I-Connecticut)

10. I support making President Bush's tax cuts permanent. But I also support the right of a woman to choose . . . I believe in immigration . . . But I also believe in the Patriot Act . . . Hillary Clinton has shortchanged New York . . . Hillary Clinton hasn't delivered. But I am not Hillary Clinton. [pause for optimal effect] You will know where I stand on the issues. Hillary Clinton [pause, much shuffling of pages, silence for 32 seconds]. Do you have page 10?

senate hopeful New York Republican Jeanine Pirro, when announcing her candidacy to the press

Unintentionally Zomboid Comments

1. Dead Man Questioned About Murder

> *headline, in a Lake Charles, Louisiana, newspaper*

2. Let's decompose and enjoy assembling!

> *instructions for a puzzle toy made in Taiwan*

3. Human Remains Found Michigan Man Gets New Hand

> *two adjoining headlines,* Valley Morning Star *(Harlingen, Texas)*

4. Q: Was Captain Cook killed on his first voyage?

   Cambridge professor Richard Porson: I believe he was, but he did not mind it much, but immediately entered on a second.

5. The Blue Jays' relief corpse isn't performing well lately.

> *Blue Jays World Series hero turned TV analyst Joe Carter*

6. Dead slow children at play

> *sign appearing on a London street*

7. Phnom Penh: Decomposed co-Prime Minister Prince Norodom Ranariddh was sentenced to 30 years imprisonment.

> The Times of India

8. **Attorney:** When was the last time you saw the deceased?
Witness: At his funeral.
Attorney: Did he make any comments to you at that time?

> *courtroom testimony*

9. Paco Park and Cemetery during the Spanish era was very much alive with dead people.

> *from an article in the Philippine magazine* What's On & Expat

10. Deaths! New! Search by surname or county. Add your own death record.

> *North Carolina BMD records*

Peculiar Classified Ads

1. 7 TOUGH GUYS NEEDED

to box against inmates in a Federal Prison. Will train, prize money to all applicants. No boxing exp. please.

help wanted ad, The Province *(Vancouver, British Columbia)*

2. Honda Civic '96. Am/FM/CD, low miles, good condition, speaks Spanish.

classified ad

3. German Shepherd 85 Lbs. Neutered. Speaks German

classified ad

4. Responsible middle-aged woman available for babysitting in her home. Potty trained.

classified ad, in a Mountain View, California, newspaper

5. Lost: Small apricot poodle— Reward. Neutered, like one of the family.

classified ad in a Florida paper

6. Brian's Psycho Service. Spring tune-up specials . . . full tune-ups as low as . . . $79.95 + parts.

> *classified ad that should have read* "Cycle *Service*"

7. Auditions: Seeking a young man who is at least 28 but not over 28 years old.

> *help wanted ad*, Hartford (Connecticut) Courant

8. Exterminating: We are trained to kill all pets.

> *classified ad*, TV Hi-Lites *(Flushing, New York)*

9. Charming Large 1 BR in beautiful Rivermont home. Meat and water incl.

> *real estate ad, in a Lynchburg, Virginia, newspaper*

10. 20 toilet rolls, hardly used, xmas bargain

> *classified ad in the* North West Evening Mail *(UK)*

THE TOP 10 STUPIDLY
Scientific Quotes

1. Scientists want to know why sex is so popular

> *headline,* Intelligencer Journal *(Lancaster, Pennsylvania)*

2. Study Finds Sex, Pregnancy Link

> *headline,* The Cornell (New York) Daily Sun

3. We don't know why, but it seems that men don't get bacterial vaginosis.

> *from a Health Education Authority leaflet on sexually transmitted diseases*

4. Animals, which move, have limbs and muscles. The earth does not have limbs or muscles. Therefore, it does not move.

> *17-century scientist Scipio Chiaramonti*

5. Panda Mating Fails; Veterinarian Takes Over

> *newspaper headline*

6. From a report on stem-cell research on paralyzed rats: For the last two years, he has shown dramatic video footage of the rats walking to scientific gatherings and during campaign events.

San Bernadino (California) Sun

7. A safe and natural alternative to silicone breast implants could be available in five years. Scientists in Boston will soon have the capacity to grow an entire breast. This news is expected to lead to a dramatic improvement in GCSE science results among 15 year old boys.

> The Guardian *(UK)*

8. International Scientific Group Elects Bimbo As Its Chairman

> *newspaper headline*

9. A study by three physicians showed that perhaps two out of three births in the U.S. result from pregnancies.

> Columbus (Ohio) Citizen

10. Larger Kangaroos Leap Farther, Researchers Find

> *headline*, Los Angeles Times

. . . And a final favorite filmic stupid word on science . . .

11. Science is science, but a girl has to have her hair done.

> *heroine scientist's final words, in* Tarantula *(1955)*

Cinematic Mad Scientists Acting Mad

1. Would you allow me to come to your house and in your presence anesthetize your wife?

> *scientist to another scientist, in* Unearthly Stranger *(1964)*

2. **Doctor:** You know, I've been working for years, developing, breeding, and conditioning these maggots. . . . They feed on human flesh.

Nazi: Why must it be human flesh? Why not animal?

Doctor: I haven't got time to explain it to you now.

> *mad doctor, discovering new scientific breakthrough, in* Flesh Feast *(1970)*

3. These [two-headed monsters] have a way of attracting attention, you know.

> *concerned scientist, to his wife after the two-headed-man-monster escapes from his lab, in* The Manster *(1959)*

4. How often have I told you to keep that cat from desecrating my graves!

> *mad doctor, to his assistant, in* Bowery at Midnight *(1942)*

5. **Dr. Hugo Wagner:** But you're sacrificing a human life!

Dr. Alfred Brandon: Do you cry over a guinea pig? This boy is a free police case. We're probably saving him from the gas chamber.

Wagner: But the boy is so young, the transformation horrible . . .

Brandon: And you call yourself a scientist! That's why you've never been anything more than an assistant!

> I Was a Teenage Werewolf *(1957)*

6. Who's going to believe a talking head? Get a job in a sideshow!

> *mad scientist, to the head of the decapitated doctor, in* Re-Animator *(1985)*

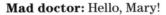

7. Young woman: Oh, here comes Dr. Carruthers! Hello, Doctor.

Mad doctor: Hello, Mary! I took a shortcut from my laboratory through a garden hedge!

> The Devil Bat *(1940)*

8. We've got two perfect specimens: a retarded man who's of no use to anyone and a homicidal maniac who'll be dead in a minute anyway. Such an opportunity may never come again!

> *lab assistant, who's just shot the maniac on the steps of the lab, realizing that the lab's retarded janitor is about to get more brain-power, in* The Incredible 2-Headed Transplant *(1971)*

9. Bride of Frankenstein: I have a life of my own—you didn't create me!

Dr. Frankenstein: As a matter of fact, I did. I sewed you together out of corpses. And I can uncreate you, too.

> *woman and mad scientist, having an argument before his hate turns to lust, in* The Bride *(1985)*

10. We're scientists. We have to do things we hate!

> *scientist, in* Curse of the Fly *(1965)*

Things Said by Women Who Professionally Pose in the Nude

Howard Stern: Define the meaning of the letters CIA:

1. Julie Cialini (1995 Playboy Playmate of the Year): I don't know.

2. Stacy Sanches (1996 Playboy Playmate of the Year): Certified Investigation Association.

Howard Stern: What is the center of our solar system?

3. Julie Cialini (1995 Playboy Playmate of the Year): The equator.

4. Stacy Sanches (1996 Playboy Playmate of the Year): The moon.

Howard Stern: Who invented the lightbulb?

5. Julie Cialini (1995 Playboy Playmate of the Year): I know Edison invented the telephone, but I can't remember the lightbulb guy.

Howard Stern: Define the NAACP.

6. **Julie Cialini (1995 Playboy Playmate of the Year):** Something, something, something, for Certified Pianists.

7. **Stacy Sanches (1996 Playboy Playmate of the Year):** It's some kind of police organization.

Howard Stern: What century are we in?

8. **Sarah, contestant for World's Strongest Naked Woman:** The 50th.

Howard Stern: What do the stars represent on the American flag?

9. **Sarah, contestant for World's Strongest Naked Woman:** They just look good.

> *during a quiz segment on* The Howard Stern Show

Howard Stern: What country did Saddam Hussein invade during the Gulf War?

10. **Sandi Korn, model/Penthouse Pet:** Uh . . . what is . . . Jerusalem?

(Sandi Korn, later): I am smart, I really am. But Howard asked me about the war and I was travelling around modeling so much that I didn't keep track of things like that. I really could have sworn that we bombed Jerusalem because I have a friend in Jerusalem and I'm sure he told me Jerusalem was bombed. But Jerusalem, Iraq—it's all the same anyway.

Things Said about Cheese (and the Top 2 Stupidest Cheese Poem Excerpts)

1. Super G String Cheese

$1.49

Buy one, get one free!

ad, Silver Spring, Maryland, supermarket flyer

2. At the Cashier's counter kindly note that personal cheese are not accepted.

helpful hint included in the in-house guidebook of the Imperial Samui Hotel in Thailand

3. AVES: Wisconsin's Finest Taxidermy & Cheese

sign on a Wisconsin store

4. *On a label of Nabisco Easy Cheese spray cheese product:*

For best results, remove cap

5. In our modern factory model the perfect curd is one that maximizes component retention but many traditional methods of manufacture used tools that did not create the perfect curd but in fact they did.

in an article on cheesereporter.com

6. This crud is from the finest milk solely from the cow's of the Brie region.

label on a French brie cheese

7. *Cheese Problems Solved*

book title

8. Aged Blue Vain Cheese

in a specialty market flyer, New York

9. Mainly made from cheese, together with colorful auxiliary material.

in a brochure for Mister Pizza Place Restaurant, Shanghai, China

10. • Fused cheese

• Head Cheese to pleasure he/she gives the victim

menu items, Mexico and Bolivia

11. Prophecy of a Ten Ton Cheese

by James McIntyre (1827–1906)

Who hath prophetic vision
   sees
In future times a ten ton
   cheese,
Several companies would join
To furnish curd for great
   combine,
More honor far than making
   gun
Of mighty size and many a
   ton.

12. Ode on the Mammoth Cheese Weighing over 7,000 Pounds

by James McIntyre

We have seen thee, queen of cheese,
Lying quietly at your ease,
Gently fanned by evening breeze,
Thy fair form no flies dare seize.

THE TOP 10 STUPIDEST

Examples of Inadvertent Irony

1. Open government seminar will be closed to the public

  Associated Press headline

2. ***The Weakest Link*** **host Anne Robinson:** In medicine, a cochlear implant is designed to enhance which of the senses?

  Contestant: Can you repeat the question, please, Anne?

3. National Collegiate Alcohol Awareness Week— Free Drinks in Student Center Lounge

  sign posted at Texas A&M– Corpus Christi

4. I just wanted to see how much of an insult it was to be called an ignoramus, since I didn't know what it meant. I just googled it. For all of you out there who don't know what an ignoramus is, it's an ignorant lawyer.

  Fox & Friends *host Gretchen Carlson*

5. Keep your government hands off my Medicare.

protest sign at a health-care reform town hall meeting in Simpsonville, South Carolina, commenting on the government-created Medicare program

6. It's always a bad practice to say "always" or "never."

President Barack Obama

7. Made in Mexico

label in U.S. Border Patrol uniforms

8. **Q:** What personality trait do you hate most in other people?
Actress Eva Longoria: Ignorance.
Q: Then what characteristic do you deplore in yourself?
Longoria: Um, wait. Deplore means to hate something, right?

9. "For Washington consultants to sit around and personally disparage the governor anonymously to reporters is unfortunate and counterproductive and frankly immature," said the aide, who spoke on condition of anonymity.

aide to Sarah Palin, commenting on Mitt Romney's staff, in a news story on Politico.com

10. Sorry. We would like to apologize to readers for the late arrival of our March issue, which was entitled "Flammable Materials : Controlling the Hazard!" The delay was caused by a fire at the printers.

apology in The Safety and Health Practitioner

Egregiously Obvious Statements Made By Politicians

1. When a storm hits, the best place to be is out of the path of the storm.

> *Secretary of Homeland Security Michael Chertoff*

2. It is indeed a great wall.

> *President Richard Nixon, while visiting the Great Wall of China*

3. Those who enter the country illegally violate the law.

> *President George W. Bush*

4. It's against the law in America to hire people illegally.

> *Sen. John Kerry (D-Massachusetts)*

5. I can only impregnate. I can't get pregnant myself.

> *Mississippi state representative Steve Holland (D-Plantersville) (Note: Steve is NOT short for "Stephanie.")*

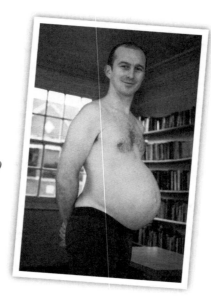

6. [This is] the most expensive redevelopment project the country has ever seen. I would think, and predict, that it is going to cost money.

Sen. Bill Frist (R-Tennessee)

7. When you're hunting for someone and you haven't found them, you haven't found them.

Defense Secretary Donald Rumsfield

8. If the Republican Party does not make substantial changes to their policies, they will largely remain the same.

Rep. Corrine Brown (D-Florida)

9. Wow! Brazil is big,

President George W. Bush, when looking at a map

10. Russia's big and so is China.

President George W. Bush

And Most Disgusting Food Items

1. The Ice Cream in Ass
   dessert menu, Russia

2. Pork with fresh garbage
   menu item, Vietnam

3. Chocolate Puke
   room service menu, White Swan Hotel in Guangzhou, China

4. Courgette fart with tomato puree
   menu item, France

5. Bacon and Germs
   menu item from the Vegetarian Restaurant, Tokyo, and other Asian restaurants

6. Spit from sharks
   menu item, Croatia

7. Pudding with scum
   menu item, Cordoba, Spain

8. Alive cancers boiled in beer on special Austrian to the recipe
   menu item, Moscow, Russia

9. Fried enema
   menu item, China

10. Herpes Grilled Tomato
   buffet item, Petra, Jordan

Newspaper and Magazine Corrections

1. A caption on the front page of Thursday's paper misidentified a room in the Department of Environmental Conservation laboratory in Juneau. The room in the photograph is the men's bathroom.

The Times *(Trenton, New Jersey)*

2. Last Sunday, The Herald erroneously reported that Dolphin Jimmy Holmes had been an insurance salesman in Raleigh, North Carolina, that he had won the New York lottery in 1982 and lost all his money in a land swindle, that he had been charged with vehicular homicide, but was acquitted because his mother said she drove the car, and that he stated that the funniest thing he ever saw was Flipper spouting water on George Wilson. Each of the items was erroneous material published inadvertently. He was not an insurance salesman  in Raleigh, he did not win the lottery, neither he nor his mother was charged with vehicular homicide, and he made no comment about Flipper or George Wilson. The Herald regrets the errors.

The Miami Herald

3. My name was printed incorrectly below my letter in the December 30 issue of the Sevenoaks Chronicle. It should read L P Pook, not L P Hook. (signed) L P Hook

Sevenoaks Chronicle *(UK)*

4. Correction: In "How to wrap a rabid rabbit" by Martin Gregory (Forum, 22 January) it was stated incorrectly that "African languages have only five vowels." It was in fact the author's "class of African students" who had only five vowels. The error was editorial and not the author's.

New Scientist

5. Correction: JoAnn Stoughter has never run a crack ring as stated in the picture caption in Tuesday's View section.

Los Angeles Times

6. In a news story Friday ("Spectrum holds Condom Olympics to educate on safe sex," page 3), it was incorrectly stated due to a reporting error that health and wellness educator Beth Grampetro and Tim Hegan, an ORL area director, said Fruit Roll-Ups are adequate protection against STDs. No health officials said or advocated this use at the Condom Olympics. *The Daily Free Press* apologizes for the confusion.

The Daily Free Press *(Boston University)*

7. The article about the Ladies' Craft Club should have stated that Mrs. Brown and Mrs. Smith gave talks on "smocking and rugs respectively," not "smoking and drugs respectably," as reported.

correction in the Althorne Village (Essex, England) News

8. A story in yesterday's *Daily* reported that SPY magazine publisher Tom Phillips said his magazine consistently refers to Donald Trump as the "short-fingered Bulgarian." The term Phillips actually used was "short-fingered vulgarian." The misquotation was not intended as a slur against Bulgarians. The *Daily* regrets the error.

> The Stanford (California) Daily

9. A news analysis article on Saturday about the politics behind Governor Pete Wilson's role in eliminating affirmative action programs at University of California campuses rendered a word incorrectly in a quotation from Sherry Bebitch Jeffe, a former legislative aide in Sacramento. Ms. Jeffe said of Mr. Wilson: "He's been biding his time on this knowing all along what he was going to do when the time was ripe. It's ripe. He's picked." She did not say, "He's pickled."

> The New York Times

10. Important Notice: If you are one of the hundreds of parachuting enthusiasts who bought out "Easy Sky Diving" book please make the following correction: on page 8, line 7, the words "state zip code" should have read "pull rip cord."

> *in a Warrenton, Virginia, newspaper*

(And Least Insightful) Football Commentaries Ever Broadcast

1. This is a home game. This is where you finally get to play at home.

sports commentator Joe Theismann

2. The Dallas Cowboys have two kinds of plays in their offense: running plays and passing plays.

sports commentator John Madden

3. The leadership definitely have to come from the leaders.

sports commentator Emmitt Smith

4. You have to do well on third downs.

sports commentator Joe Buck

5. The Giants will have to play physical football to beat the Panthers.

sports commentator Daryl Johnston

6. The winner of this game is going to be whoever has the most points on the scoreboard at the end of the game.
sports commentator John Madden

7. It's hard to matriculate the ball.
sports commentator John Lynch

8. Don't worry about the game you just won or the team that we just blew out . . . or, um . . . blown . . . blowed out . . . Let's think about what we need to do going forward, and they had, uh . . . blown out.
sports commentator Emmitt Smith

9. That was a well-executed play that they didn't execute very well.
sports commentator Kirk Herbstreit

10. You gotta score to put points on the board.
sports commentator Joe Theismann

Modern Medical Definitions

1. Mental activity at the margins:
   insanity

2. Therapeutic misadventure:
   medical malpractice

3. Hematophagous arthropod vectors:
   fleas

4. Aggravated bovine ejection:
   being bucked off of a bull

5. Negative Patient Care Outcome:
   death

6. Immediate Permanent Incapacitation:
   death

7. Chronologically Experienced Citizens:
   elderly people

8. Compensated Edentia:
   false teeth

9. Nutritional Avoidance Therapy:
   diet

10. Thermal Remediation Unit:
    ice bag

    definitions used in medical reports

THE TOP 10 STUPIDEST
"Oh, Shut Up"
Quotes

1. I think it's impossible to live in a room which isn't at least 13 feet high. Don't you?

> *jewelry designer Kenneth Jay Lane, in an interview in which he showed off his apartment*

2. I really know how to think. If I decide to make a coat red in the show, it's not just red. I think: Is it communist red? Is it cherry cordial? Is it ruby red? Or is it apple red? Or the big balloon red? I mean there's so many f***ing different kinds of red. And so you have to say, well, what are we trying to say in this scene? Is it a happy red? Or a sad red? Is it a lace red? Or a leather red? Or a wool red?

> *singer Lady Gaga, explaining how her education at her high school— the Convent of the Sacred Heart in Manhattan—helped her think well*

3. Q: What have been your most memorable London meals?

Actress Emily Mortimer: Mezzo with producer Stephen Evans. He suggested champagne to cure my hangover. He then asked if I could write a treatment for Lorna Sage's Bad Blood. Afterwards I vomited copiously outside Our Price. It was a prelapsarian moment, but now it seems quite portentous.

> *in a magazine interview*

4. A really good friend said to me, "I always thought you were like a beautiful lacquered box with a silver handle. Now I know there is something inside the box." Nobody said these things to me before.

> *fashion designer Tom Ford*

5. Even when I was having my hair and makeup done backstage at a fashion show, I would sneak in a copy of Dostoyevsky and read it inside a copy of *Elle* or *Vogue*. But it would be pretentious of me to say I was more intelligent than the other supermodels of that era. I was always just curious about everything.

former model and French first lady Carla Bruni

6. It took all my semiotic Lacanian deconstructivist saturation and torqued it.

film director Kathryn Bigelow

7. No one buys a Big Mac for the simple reasons of eating it. The behavior is part of an entire gestalt in which the consumer participates on a subliminal level. The purchase of a Big Mac involves a deep interior perception of self, family, country and socio-economic status.

Michael R. Steele, author of an essay about McDonald's

8. Yoko Ono: Did you ever hear the story about three pots of plants? Three pots of plants, each watered with certain thoughts: One watered with nothing, just water, the other watered with love and the other with hate. Which do you think grew better?

Indie Rocker Beth Ditto: Love.

Yoko: Well, you think that, don't you? Hate and love was equal, and the one you didn't do anything about died.

9. I get up to leave. "I'll show you out a different way," she says. We walk through an atrium painted in pale pink, with huge silver doors leading out of her flat. "I designed it myself," she says. "It represents the womb. The doors are the labia, and this," she points to the corridor, "is the birth canal."

actress Jane Fonda, interviewed by Emma Brockes in
The Guardian *(UK)*

10. Q: What is a phrase you use far too often?

Designer Peter Saville: Post-war socio-culture democratization. It's my rationale for everything.

The Independent *(UK)*

Quotes from the Department of Redundancy Department

1. I don't make predictions, especially those considering the future.

  Bloc Québécois leader Gilles Duceppe

2. PIZZA HUT
We Have Pizza!

  ad outside a Pizza Hut

3. It's not as cold as it was yesterday, but that's probably because it's a bit warmer.

  sportscaster Ian Botham

4. The internet is a great way to get on the net.

  Sen. Bob Dole (R-Kansas)

5. You're going to see some never-before-seen footage that you've never seen before.

  rocker Bret Michaels, about his reality show

6. Our nation must come together to unite.

  President George W. Bush

7. Sanguillen is totally unpredictable to pitch to because he's so unpredictable.

San Diego Padres broadcaster Jerry Coleman

8. I don't like to look back in retrospect.

football player Vince Ferragamo

9. We have very hazardous conditions due to a five-year drought, and lack of rain hasn't helped any, either.

KABC-7 reporter, Los Angeles

10. This is all about historical events in the past.

British prime minister Tony Blair

Statements about Heaven, Hell, Demons, and Angels

1. This is the gate of Heaven. Enter ye all by this door. (This door is kept locked because of the draft. Please use side entrance.)

sign on a church door

2. Harewood Christian Discussion Group: We shall be meeting on Wednesday, 11th April when the subject will be "Heaven. How do we get there?" Transport is available at 7:55pm from the bus stop opposite the Harewood Arms.

from the Collingham parish magazine (England)

3. The sermon at the Presbyterian Church this coming Sunday will be "There Are No Sects in Heaven." The subject was incorrectly printed in yesterday's edition as "There Is No Sex in Heaven."

newspaper correction

4. The Playing of Ball Games

Riding of Cycles

Exorcising of Dogs

Strictly Prohibited

sign in a park, Pendle, Lancashire (England)

5. **Game show host Jeff Owen:** Who invented the telescope and the thermometer?

Contestant: [pause] Er . . . .

Owen: Think of "Bohemian Rhapsody" by Queen and you'll get it.

Contestant: Beelzebub?

Notts and Crosses, BBC Radio Nottingham *(England)*

6. **Game show host William "G" Stewart:** Above the entrance to which place do the words "Abandon all hope, ye who enter here" appear?

Contestant: A church?

on the game show Fifteen to One *(UK)*

7. Travelsupplies.com provides you with all the electrical, telephone and computer requirements you'll need when traveling to Hell.

ad for Travelsupplies.com

8. I see hell in hello. It's disguised by the o, but once you see it, it will slap you in the face.

flea market operator Leonso Canales of Kingsville, Texas, on his county-supported campaign to change "hello" to "heaveno"

9. I am not losing my daughter to a 900-year-old goat's head!

mom defending her daughter, who is possessed by Mexican demons, in Dolly Dearest *(1992)*

10. If Christ came to Sydney today, he would be on "the Hill" at cricket matches driving home the lessons of the game. One can imagine Christ reminding the crowd that Satan was the deadliest and most determined googly bowler of all time.

Rev. T. McVittie, moderator of the Sydney, Australia, Presbytery during the 1930s

Injury Insights

1. ***The Weakest Link* host Anne Robinson:** A pain in the muscles or bones of the lower legs, often suffered by sportsmen, is known as shin . . . ?

Contestant: . . . dler's List.

2. And he's got the icepack on his groin there, so it's possibly not the old shoulder injury . . .

sportscaster Ray French

3. We knew Jermaine wasn't injured. He was just hurt a little bit.

basketball player Ron Artest, after Jermaine O'Neal's knee injury in the playoffs

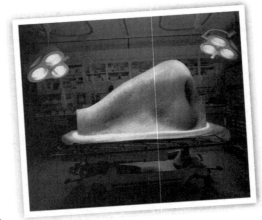

4. I think he got the stick in the nose. He broke his nose earlier, and it looks as though it's the same nose that he injured before.

CBS sports announcer, during a hockey game on "Game of the Week"

5. Sonny Liston has a very unusual injury—a dislocated soldier.

BBC sportscaster Henry Cooper, on the historic Sonny Liston–Muhammad Ali fight

6. Bleeding started in the rectal area and continued all the way to Los Angeles.

patient chart notes, written by a health-care provider, as printed in Frontier Healthcare's "Details in Professional Liability" newsletter

7. Winter-related injuries occur more often in the winter.

newswoman, WHIZ-TV, Zanesville, Ohio

8. It's only puffy when it's swollen.

baseball player Charlie Hough, on his broken finger

9. Danny, as you know, was hospitalized last week after complaining about chest and sideburns.

sportscaster Ned Martin, doing radio play-by-play coverage of a Red Sox game

10. Reporter: What's the story on your eye infection?

Basketball player Kenny Thomas: It's in the back of my eye. I think it's the rectum.

Ridiculously Overwrought and Annoying Critical Commentary

1. Like a lot of people, as soon as I got my copy of Sarah Palin's "Going Rogue," I immediately thought of the German literary critic Hans Robert Jauss.

> *journalist Matthew Continetti,*
> *in* The Washington Post

2. But this book is about big things—friendship, motherhood, love, loss— seen through the prism of smoke from a joss stick, set to jingly jangly music that still makes the hair on the back of my neck stand up, produces a shiver not unlike that from a Fox's glacier mint, and makes me almost, but not quite, want to wet my pants.

> *critic Liz Jones, on the novel* I Think I Love You,
> *by Allison Pearson*

3. If you read his work today, you can see literary semen spraying across the American century.

> *columnist Johann Hari on the legacy of Jack London,*
> *in* The Independent *(UK)*

4. Tarantino's question remains, and remains unanswered. What *did* Travolta *do?* . . . In the firmament, the brightest stars have the shortest lives: blue giant to black hole. But the universe isn't old enough to encompass the degeneration which Travolta managed. It will take 20 billion years for our sun to reach its ultimate state, frozen in crystalline indetectability. Travolta did it in 10.

> *novelist Martin Amis, in an interview with John Travolta for the* Sunday Times *(UK) magazine*

5. Believe me, trapeze school was Mary-Kate's idea. I had emailed her a few days before and suggested we see the Philip Glass opera *Satyagraha* at the Met or peruse the Christian Louboutin show at the FIT museum. "I don't know," she tells me now, handing the release form back to the receptionist. "I was sitting in China, and I thought: trapeze class!" That one sentence—absurdly fabulous and fearless at once—pretty much sums up this 22-year-old child-woman in my presence.

> *journalist Kevin Sessums, in an interview with actress Mary-Kate Olson*

6. Time, as Proust taught us, may be a measure thing, but it is ultimately something we experience subjectively. No one in tennis makes us more aware of Proust's insight than Rafael Nadal.

> *on the* New York Times *tennis blog*

7. The launch of a new Chanel nail color is an event, much in the way the birth of a child is. . . .

> *fashion critic, in the* Observer *(UK) magazine, Life and Style section*

8. Having famously rhymed "al fresco" with "Tesco," [Lily Allen] offers, in a new track about God, the following couplet: "Do you think He's ever been suicidal?/His favorite band is Creedence Clearwater Revival." Only in England could such a line be written or, indeed, relished.

journalist Matthew d'Ancona, from an article about musician Lily Allen, in the Spectator *(UK)*

9. As Federer glides around the court, flicking forehands and caressing backhand, I guess I am not the only one who is put in mind of Tennyson, "All experience is an arch wherethrough gleams that untravelled world. . . ."

journalist Matthew Syed, in The Times *(UK)*

10. It would not have surprised me to have seen the credits of Toy Story 3 announce: "Based on an original idea by Albert Camus and Jean-Paul Sartre." True, you cannot imagine a Camus character being called Lots-o-Huggin Bear, but you can imagine the great French existentialist penning sobering lines such as "We're all trash waiting to be thrown away," and "You think you're special? You're just a piece of plastic."

critic Julian Baggini, The Times *(UK)*

Fast-Food Fails

1. Try a 50 year old
Whopper with Cheese!

sign outside a Burger King (advertising the fact that the Whopper had been invented 50 years before)

2. What's the difference between the small, the medium, and the large? The size?

woman at a Wendy's drive-thru window

3. McDonald's customer: I'd like the breakfast—A.
Cashier: Do you mean the number A or the letter A?

conversation in a New York City McDonald's

4. Fast Food This Way
Oral Cholera available

two signs adjacent to each other, Manila

5. 0 Piece Chicken Nuggets 5.99

sign for Fast Food Restaurant

6. Try Our New Anus Burger

sign at McDonald's, Kalamazoo, Michigan

7. Try a steak beagle for breakfast today

sign at McDonald's, Minneapolis, Minnesota

8. **McDonald's customer:** How many McNuggets come in a Six Piece?

Counterperson: Six.

Customer: Oh, that's what I thought.

   conversation in a McDonald's restaurant

9. Drive-Thru Parking Only

   sign at McDonald's in Ocean City

10. We Don't Just Serve Hamburgers,
We Serve People!

   on a Burger King employment application

Examples of Celebrities Sharing Their Vast Knowledge

1. I love Africa in general, South Africa and West Africa. They are both great countries.

> *socialite Paris Hilton*

2. I've never really wanted to go to Japan simply because I don't really like eating fish, and I know that's very popular out there in Africa.

> *singer Britney Spears*

3. Chemistry is a class you take in high school or college where you figure out $2 + 2 = 10$ or something.

> *basketball player Dennis Rodman*

4. Our offense is like the Pythagorean theorem: There is no answer!

> *basketball player Shaquille O'Neal*

5. [I] don't eat lobster or anything like that cause they're alive when you kill it.

> Jersey Shore *reality star Snooki*

6. **Reporter:** Do you read Kierkegaard?

> **Actress Pamela Anderson:** Uh, what movies was he in?

7. My boyfriend gave me [a necklace with a tiny circle on it reminiscent of a planet] because it was our first-year anniversary and it takes like a year for the sun to rotate around the earth.

> *actress Kirsten Dunst*

8. You can hardly tell where the computer models finish and the real dinosaurs begin.

> *actress Laura Dern,*
> *on* Jurassic Park

9. **Costar of *Rich Girls* Jaime Gleicher:** We must have done something really good for us to have the privileges that we do. Benjamin Franklin was born on my birthday. Muhammad Ali was born on my birthday. Like, maybe I was one of them.

Costar of *Rich Girls* Ally Hilfiger: Who? Who was born on your birthday?

Gleicher: Benjamin Franklin—who invented the lightbulb.

> *on an episode of* Rich Girls, *reality show about, you guessed it,*
> *two rich girls: Ally Hilfiger (daughter of designer Tommy Hilfiger)*
> *and Jaime Gleicher*

10. **Interviewer:** Are you attending the Cannes film festival this year?
Singer Christina Aguilera: I hope so. Where is it being held this year?

Criminally Idiotic Moments

1. **Defense attorney:** Are you sure you did not enter the 7-11 on 40th and Northeast Broadway and hold up the cashier on June 17 of this year?

Defendant: I'm pretty sure.

comments taken from court records

2. My son couldn't have been involved [in the drive-by shooting] because, at exactly ten-thirty, when this shooting took place, he was over the other side of town in a housing project, murdering someone who owed us money.

a New Orleans woman, defending her son to the police, who were accusing him of having committed a drive-by shooting

3. **Judge:** You say you're innocent, yet five people swore they saw you steal a watch.

Defendant: Your Honor, I can produce 500 people who didn't see me steal it.

courtroom testimony

4. Give me $418—and no ones.

bank robber in Dundalk, Maryland, to a bank teller

5. **Detective [surveying a lineup]:** Now each of you repeat the words "Give me all your money or I'll shoot."

Suspect in the lineup: That's not what I said!

6. Judge: You have a right to a trial by jury, but you may waive that right.

Defendant: [Thinking, says nothing]

Lawyer to defendant: Waive.

Defendant: [Waves at judge.]

courtroom testimony

7. Man in bank line (Philadelphia): I am a bank robber. Give me the money.

Man behind man in bank line: I am a policeman. You are under arrest.

8. <u>To Do List</u>

- Clean tubs, sink, counter, and toilets
- Get ski mask
- Get police scanner
- Find escape route
- Borrow gun from someone

list found by police and written by Elizabeth Maddex, 19-year-old former cheerleader who later pled guilty to robbing a bank in California

9. Judge: The charge here is theft of frozen chickens. Are you the defendant, sir?

Defendant: No, sir. I'm the guy who stole the chickens.

Comments taken from court records

10. Police officer (to purse-snatching suspect in lineup): Put your baseball cap on the other way, with the bill facing front.

Suspect: No, I'm gonna put it on backwards. That's the way I had it on when I took the purse.

Film Cop Moments

1. You may know about corpses, fella, but you've got a lot to learn about women.

> *policeman to morgue worker, in* Autopsy *(1975)*

2. This criminal must be found. Otherwise, these acts will continue!

> *cop, in* Wrestling Women vs. the Aztec Ape *(1962)*

3. Monsters, space people, mad doctors. They didn't teach me about such things at the police academy.

> *Officer Kelton, in* Night of the Ghouls *(1959)*

4. Show me a crime and I'll show you the dirty picture that caused it!

> *cop about porno's effect, in* The Sinister Urge *(1960)*

5. One thing's sure. Inspector Clay's dead. Murdered. . . . And somebody's responsible!

> *police officer, in* Plan 9 from Outer Space *(1959)*

6. I'll have to see him before I believe he's invisible.

> *policeman who doesn't quite know what to believe, in* The Invisible Man Returns *(1940)*

7. **Cop #1:** Did you get anything out of her?

Cop #2: True, she was frightened and in a state of shock. But don't forget, she tore her nightgown and had scratched feet.

Cop #1: Yeah, I hadn't thought of that.

   Plan 9 from Outer Space *(1959)*

8. **Psychiatrist:** You're referring to the suicide of the transvestite?

Policeman: If that's the word you men of medical science use for a man who wears women's clothing, yes.

   Glen or Glenda *(1953)*

9. He makes me feel like a moron—but I like him.

   police chief, discussing the Venusian who has come to Earth, in Stranger from Venus *(1954)*

10. I'll tell you what it is, Fanducci. It's a big guy in a bulletproof dog suit. I know a serial killer when I see one.

   top cop Chief Richardson, to his detective, in The Runestone *(1991)*

"Close but No Cigar" Foreign Signs

1. Please Steek Gently.

> *sign on recreational hall for foreign immigrants, Taipei, Taiwan*

2. No Smonking

> *sign, China*

3. Please do not be a dog.

> *sign on grass in a Paris park*

4. Do not open your face to monkeys.

> *sign at mountainside rest area near Nikko, Japan*

5. Please do not feed the animals. If you have any suitable food, give it to the guard on duty.

> *sign at a Budapest zoo*

6. Hotel Bar. No drinking prohibited.

> *sign in Turkish cocktail lounge*

7. All items or staff can black or difficult the way will be remove of the fire escapes.
All the staff will be put on the basement for 2 days.

> *sign in an office building, Spain*

8. Beware of safety.

road sign, Suzhou, China

9. Cars will not have Intercourse on this Bridge.

Tokyo traffic sign

10. Please do not invade Madame's private parts.

sign posted in French château that rented rooms to tourists,
intending to warn against trespassing in the owners' private rooms

. . . And 3 Completely Uninterpretable Foreign Signs

1. Cement Should Hear.

sign in India (that was intended to say "cement sold here")

2. The Thing Tube Office

English-language sign on a door, China (the Chinese characters
underneath just say "Office")

3. Please Blance

sign, China

Double Entendres

1. Mom Blows Lucy's Date

>*headline on the "Dear Abby" column in the* Parkersburg (West Virginia) Sentinel

2. *Female TV news anchor to male weatherman regarding snowfall amounts:*

>Where's that six inches you promised me last night?

>*on a Nebraska news show*

3. Notices are appearing at courses telling golfers not to lick their balls on the green.

>*commentator Richie Benaud, during a British Masters tournament*

4. Sir, I have been fingering your waitress for a long time, but she just does not want to come.

>*Joseph "Erap" Estrada, vice president of the Philippines, complaining to a restaurant manager when a waitress ignored his gestures and failed to come over to the table*

5. **Yankees player's wife:** When my husband's away, I have to take charge of everything. I have to be pretty much the man in the family.

Sportscaster Jerry Coleman: Yes, I suppose you do have to wear the pants in the family at this time.

Wife: Yes, but when he comes home, I take them off.

> *conversation during a postgame television show, following a New York Yankees–Baltimore Orioles game*

6. Choir Director Shows His Organ to New Church Women

> Morning Herald *(Gloversville, New York)*

7. Canadians get helping hand during sperm crisis

> *headline,* Sunday Herald *(UK)*

8. There's two lovers in the stands. He kisses her on the strikes and she kisses him on the balls.

> *Minnesota Twins sportscaster, during a lull in the game when the camera was taking shots of people in the stands*

9. . . . and now he catches the puck and rams it between the girlie's legs and scores . . . of course, I meant goalie.

> *Boston sportscaster, during a hockey game*

10. Fewer Balls, more Wangs as British names change: Researchers study surnames

> *Reuters headline*

Moments in Live Broadcasting

1. They've got a teletepathic, teletepathic, pathetic, well, it's not pathetic . . . oh, just forget it.

   broadcaster Graham Taylor

2. J.Lo's new song "Jenny from the Block" is all about Lopez's roots, about how she's still a neighborhood gal at heart. But folks from that street in New York, the Bronx section, sound more likely to give her a curb job than a blow job!

   Fox newscaster Shepard Smith (he quickly tried to correct himself by adding "or a bl-bl-block party")

3. Newscaster Michael Peschardt: Laura, what can you tell us about [spy agency] MI2's involvement?

   Field reporter (on site): Not a lot. They're a fairly secretive organization.

   interchange on BBC Breakfast *(UK)*

4. Bozo the Clown: You're never a loser on the Bozo show, you're just an almost-winner.

   Kid, who has just lost the prize: Cram it, clown.

   during a live broadcast of the Bozo the Clown *show*

5. Newscaster Krishnan Gury-Murthy: So, Simon, what do you know?

   Reporter Simon Israel: Well, not a lot, to be honest.

   Channel 4 News (UK)

6. One man in particular here in Santa Ana knows full well the story—and he has lived it and he knows how these immigrants feel. . . . We don't have the tape ready, but I can tell you the tape comes from a man named Jose Vargas and I'll just go with the whim of the desk—You can tell me—we, we do have the tape—OK. This is the tape from one man's viewpoint . . . Well, we still don't have that tape. I understand, so the man's name is Jose Vargas, who is a police officer, who also was an und—We do have the tape? I'm just at the mercy of the booth. Do we have the tape or not? I'm sorry. Uh, uh, I, I assume we do have the—We don't have the tape, all right let me explain the story again. We'll try it one more time. Jose Vargas is a man who works—we do have the tape. Let's go to the tape. . . . No tape. OK.

broadcaster Dave Lopez, KCBS-TV (Los Angeles)

7. Here comes the Royal Family now. The automobile has now stopped, a member of the RCMP is opening the car door—oh, there's the King—he's stepping out, followed by her Majesty Queen Elizabeth, nattily attired in a silver coat. Mr. King is now shaking hands with the King and introducing Mr. Queen to the King and Queen and then Mrs. Queen to the Queen and King. They are now proceeding up the steps to the well-decorated City Hall, the King and Mr. King together with the Queen being escorted by Mrs. Queen. The King has now stopped and said something to Mrs. Queen and goes to Mrs. Queen and the Queen and Mr. King and the Queen laughed jovially. The King leaves Mr. King and goes to Mrs. Queen and the Queen and Mr. King follow behind . . .

a Canadian Broadcasting Corporation radio announcer doing his best to give a coherent on-the-spot report of the 1939 visit of King George VI and his wife to Winnipeg—and their meeting with the Canadian prime minister, Mackenzie King, and the mayor of Winnipeg, John Queen, and his wife, Mrs. Queen

8. As you might have heard, NewsChannel 5 is throwing a big Halloween party tonight, and our own Beth Basen joins us [pause] is Beth with us? [pause] Alrighty, evidently we do not have that picture right now. We will bring it to you later, okay? Okay. Now I'm told we have it back. Now that's the way things seem in the television business with us. Okay, now we go to John who's live outside the old train depot downtown. John, how're things going down there? [shot of John talking with no audio] Alrighty, we evidently don't have any audio with John there. John thinks he does, but he actually doesn't. Um, we'll check back in with him later. Thanks, John.

And you may be wondering why these people are bashing this car in with a sledgehammer? Well actually you can't see that right now, but they did it. We'll have that story and more. All right, I might be asking for trouble by doing this, but let's go back to the train depot downtown and see if we can talk to John Martin who's down there at NewsChannel 5's big Halloween party. John, are you there? [no audio] [pause] We can still not hear him, so we won't try that any more. You're watching NewsChannel 5 at 10.

TV anchorman, during a nightly news show

9. **Newscaster #1:** Now Mike and I are working today—and how do you feel about working today, Mike?

Newscaster #2: I'm Dave.

10. **Radio 5 Live:** What's it like in Athens tonight, Roger?

Gold medalist Roger Black: Actually, I'm not in Athens, but in the front room of a friend's house in Guildford. I've been dropped from the BBC team in Athens.

Radio 5 Live interview on the Athens Olympics

Answers

1. **Reporter:** Is it difficult to find your way around Tampa Bay?
Soccer player Thomas Ravelli: No, as long as you don't get lost.

2. **Attorney:** What do you do for a living?
Witness: I help my brother.
Attorney: What does your brother do?
Witness: Nothing.
> *courtroom testimony*

3. **Reporter:** What do you think were the signs that you would win the election?
Waukesha County Circuit Court judicial winner Paul Reilly: We concentrated heavily on yard signs. And yard signs, particularly, in people's yards.

4. **Q:** How can you tell the age of a snake?
A: It is extremely difficult to tell the age of a snake unless you know exactly when it was born.
> *in a nature questions column*, The Detroit News

5. **Reporter:** Why do you think you've been reincarnated?
Singer Lee Ryan: Every time I eat chicken I eat it with my hands . . . like they did in the olden days.

6. **Question on insurance form:** Could either driver have done anything to avoid the accident?
Insurance claimant's answer: Traveled by bus?

7. **Lawyer:** James shot Tommy Lee?
Witness: Yes.
Lawyer: Then Tommy Lee pulled out his gun and shot James in the fracas?
Witness: No sir, just above it.
courtroom testimony

8. **Tech support:** Are you reading an error message to me?
Customer: No, I'm reading an error message to you.

9. **Q:** How may slightly soiled playing cards be cleaned?
A: They are made by stringing pieces of meat, quarters of onions, and two-inch pieces of bacon on sticks and broiling them over coals.
in a homemaking magazine

10. **Q:** What's your reaction to hitting a grand slam?
Baseball player Garry Maddox: As I remember it, the bases were loaded.

THE TOP 10 STUPIDEST
Bold Stances

1. **Reporter:** Would you have gone to war against Saddam Hussein if he refused to disarm?

Sen. John Kerry (D-Massachusetts) (then campaigning for the presidency): You bet we might have.

2. **New York governor Mario Cuomo:** If an offer [for an appointment on the Supreme Court] were made, I would answer the question so swiftly that every one of you in the media, and especially talk-show hosts, would write, "This, surely, is the most decisive man in America."

Reporter: Would you accept the offer?

Cuomo: I don't know what the answer would be.

3. I've never been so certain about anything in my life. I want to be a coach or a manager, I'm not sure which.
> *soccer player Phil Neville*

4. **Reporter:** Would you quit baseball if the Yankees lose the series to the Pirates?

N.Y. Yankees manager Casey Stengel: Well, I have given that thought a lot of thinking lately and last night, well—finally made up my mind.

Reporter: Which way?

Stengel: I made up my mind both ways.
> *Stengel, at a press conference before a decisive World Series game*

5. I think some of the steps I've taken were slightly bold.
> *Sen. John Warner (R-Virginia), defending his record in the Senate*

6. **President George H. W. Bush:** Let me be clear, I'm not in favor of new taxes. I'll repeat that over and over and over again. And this one compromise that—where we begrudgingly had to accept revenue, revenue increases, is the exception that proves the rule . . .

Reporter: The exception that proves what rule?

Bush: The rule that I'm strongly opposed to raising taxes.

7. I actually did vote for the $87 billion, before I voted against it.

Sen. John Kerry (D-Massachusetts), on voting against a military funding bill for U.S. troops in Iraq

8. **Rep. Bill Young's (R-Florida) speech in Congress:** The B-52 has been an effective war machine. It's killed a lot of people.

Rep. Bill Young's speech as officially recorded in the *Congressional Record*—after staffers complained that he sounded too warlike: The B-52 has been an effective war machine, which has unfortunately killed a lot of people.

9. **Financial reporter:** Do you think we should repeal the Bush tax cuts?

Sen. Hillary Clinton (D-New York): I'm not sure that that's exactly what we should do, but I think the combination of fiscal responsibility and economic growth proves to be very positive for our country.

10. I'm not indecisive. Am I indecisive?

St. Paul mayor Jim Scheibel

About the Authors

Kathryn and **Ross Petras,** brother and sister, are the specialists in stupidity whose *365 Stupidest Things Ever Said* Page-A-Day® calendar has over 4 million copies in print. Their other books include *"Dance First. Think Later"*; *"Age Doesn't Matter Unless You're a Cheese"*; and *"Don't Forget to Sing in the Lifeboats."* Kathryn Petras lives in Manhattan with her husband; Ross Petras lives in Toronto with his family.

Photo Credits

age fotostock: Actionplus p. 19, Alexander Wurditsch p. 42; **Associated Press:** p. 96; **Fotolia:** Andy Dean p. 2, Joniva p. 21, Robert Lehmann p. 18, photo-dave p. 7; **Getty Images:** p. 30, p. 67, p. 71, p. 78, p. 176, AFP p. 4, p. 86, altrendo images p. 55, p. 57, Dirk Anschutz p. 63, Archive Holdings Inc. p. 10, p. 144, p. 157, Austrian Archives (S)/Imagno p. 114, James Baigrie p. 38, Christian Baitg p. 187, Nick Ballon p. 135, Barry p. 95, Michael Blann p. 226, Tim Bradley p. 82, p. 106, Philip J Brittan p. 184, Steve Bronstein p. 213, Chris Butler p. 138, Greg Ceo p. 165, Maurizio Cigognetti p. 59, Michael Cogliantry p. 219, Steve Cole p. 223, Andy Crawford p. 202, Max Dannenbaum p. 108, Peter Dazeley p. 164, John Drysdale p. 113, Rebecca Emery p. 119, Brian Erler p. 195, Evening Standard p. 103, Felbert + Eickenberg/STOCK4B p. 204, Bob Ferris p. 153, Tim Flach p. 143, Fox Photos p. 166, Jerry Gay p. 47, General Photographic Agency p. 178, Ken Harding/BIPs p. 125, Martha Holmes p. 85, Mark Hooper p. 180, Hulton Archive p. 133, p. 170, Imagno p. 32, Thomas Jackson p. 151, Jupiterimages p. 110, Keith Seaman-Camerad Inc p. 79, Sian Kennedy p. 92, Don Klumpp p. 25, Peter Kramer p. 155, Harry Langdon p. 115, Gene Lester p. 13, Berchin Maclean p. 161, George Marks p. 75, George Marks/Retrofile p. 168, Patrick McDonogh p. 206, Ethan Miller p. 174, Francis Miller/Time Life Pictures p. 134, Joos Mind p. 69, Mistik Pictures p. 200, ML Harris p. 80, Karen Moskowitz p. 128, Sean Murphy p. 44, Erin Patrice O'Brien p. 20, Orlando p. 36, Silvia Otte p. 121, Meredith Parmelee p. 88, Bec Parsons p. 51, Thomas Prior p. 214, Retrofile p. 40, Jim Ross p. 126, Andy Sacks p. 193, Stephen Saks p. 105, Adrian Samson p. 117, Joel Sartore p. 65, Sylvia Serrado p. 140, Peter Sherrard p. 190, Chip Simons p. 188, SuperStock p. 14, p. 16, p. 196, p. 221, Paul Taylor p. 137, Paul Thomas p. 61, Time & Life Pictures p. 24, Tooga p. 131, Donald Uhrbrock/Time Life Pictures p. 229, Miguel Villagran p. 147, Vintage Images p. 8, p. 149, p. 208, Shoko Yukitake p. 90; **Photofest:** p. 217, Empire Pictures p. 183, © Something Weird Video p. 101.